Terrorism or Patriotism

Terrorism or Patriotism

A PRIMER ON UNDERSTANDING CONFLICT IN THE MIDDLE EAST

Dr. Hensley J. Hunter

Front Cover: David with the Head of Goliath
               Guido Reni, 1605
               Oil on canvas, 220 X 145 cm
               Musée du Louvre, Paris

Copyright © 2007 by Dr. Hensley J. Hunter.

ISBN: Softcover   978-1-4257-7088-4

All rights reserved. No part of this book may be reproduced or transmitted in any form or by any means, electronic or mechanical, including photocopying, recording, or by any information storage and retrieval system, without permission in writing from the copyright owner.

This book was printed in the United States of America.

To order additional copies of this book, contact:
Xlibris Corporation
1-888-795-4274
www.Xlibris.com
Orders@Xlibris.com
39777

Contents

Preface 7

1. The Abuse of Terminology by Spin and Slogans 11
2. The Machiavellian Way of Politics and Governance 18
3. Early History of Terrorism in Israel-Palestine 24
4. The Conspiracy of Silence and the Rise of Arafat 34
5. The Widespread Presence of Terrorism in our Time 38
6. The Iranian Problem: How Obdurate Is It? 56
7. The Theory of "The Double Solution" 60
8. The Need for American Impartiality 64
9. Terrorism or Patriotism: Regional Differences 68
10. The Present Condition of the West 73
11. Terrorism and Patriotism as Religious Reactions 77
12. Neocons, Christian Zionists, and Brinksmanship 81
13. Where there is an Honest Will there is a Way 93
14. Pope Benedict XVI on the Use of Reason 99
15. Working Towards a Peaceful World 102

Bibliography 105

Preface

It took me one month to write the first draft for this book. What I have written is ordinary knowledge to me because it has been part of my observation and analysis for over seventy years (since I was nineteen). Some of it goes against the grain of the political correctness touted daily in the news media. But my perception is representative of the prevalent view among those Middle Eastern intellectuals who love America and have graduated from its universities, but who think that American Foreign policy in that region is embarked on a course detrimental to its own best interests. It is also a view tempered by my having lived in that region for several decades before returning to the United States, and by having traveled there frequently ever since.

A change of course in our foreign policy towards the Middle East will bring us surprisingly fast beneficial results from an area where we are presently despised. I firmly believe this. Unfortunately, I remember what H. L. Mencken once said: "The men the American people admire most extravagantly are the most daring liars; the men they detest most violently are those who try to tell them the truth." I am taking that risk in writing honestly as a philosopher and a historian about historical facts that contradict many of the false impressions that the average American has of the Middle Eastern scene.

This book is a primer for the person who knows little about the history of the Middle East, and knows even less about what took place in that area of the world during the past century. It will also inform those who believe they know the politics of the area because of what they hear analyzed daily in the news media. Some of what I say may contradict the committed beliefs of certain friends whom I respect and cherish. Both Jew and Arab, terrorist and patriot, Moslem and Christian, conservative and liberal, fundamentalist and traditionalist, may not agree with certain statements I make. Nonetheless, I write honestly in an attempt to modify mind-sets that have been hardened by holding the same opinions (garnered from the same news media) year-after-year. A modification in our thinking process, both East and West, is paramount if we are to hope for political and social improvements in that fragile area.

I have loved Western Culture since childhood. But my greatest passion has been for classical European music and its history. I am continuously amazed at the number and virtuosity of European Jewish violinists, pianists and conductors, both here and in Europe, whose concerts I have attended over the span of my life. I have heard in person Heifetz, Elman, Menuhin and Milstein play the violin in my youth. I have attended concerts of Serkin, Rubinstein, Horowitz and Barenboim and marveled at their genius. I have heard Bruno Walter conduct Mahler, Koussevitsky perform Mendelssohn, and Bernstein interpreting Gershwin and Meyerbeer. As a child I learned of Einstein's $E=mc^2$, and in graduate school I was introduced to Feynman's pyrotechnics in mathematical theory. What a brilliant race! What a highly distinguished culture, frequently in the forefront of invention and innovation! And in social action too, its people have proven to be compassionate and understanding of the needs of the disadvantaged minorities within our country, and have fought frequently for their cause.

One can fathom the perspective of a horde of uneducated religious extremists descending on the six-million technically and culturally advanced population of Israel and bringing it to an end. It would be civilization's great loss, as well as the annihilation of a good part of art and science in the Middle East. Israel is a beacon of intellectual light in that region. Only madmen would desire its elimination. It has a right to arm itself and be vigilant. And yet the ruling classes, the *politicos*, of Israel leave a lot to be desired. These leftovers from the early days of Zionism live and act as a different breed compared to the talented Jews I mention above, and to the Jewish friends I have come to appreciate and respect over the years. Could it be the weight of office and its responsibilities that cause Israel's ruling class to be so blind to the plight of their immediate neighbors, the Palestinians? Would the fear of another holocaust make that ruling class heartless, with no compassion for any antagonist be it Palestinian, Lebanese, or Syrian? They frequently extract ten eyes for an eye, and a whole body for a hand. It would appear that these people belong to a different race from the Jewish people whose friendship I have learned to love and treasure in the United States and overseas throughout my life.

On the other side of the coin, our American family lived side by side with Christians, Moslems and Jews during my adolescent years in the Middle East. I remember them as peaceful, friendly and hospitable. For several years, when my parents worked overseas for our State Department, I attended both Christian and Moslem schools. I read the Koran every day in class (it was mandatory) and I didn't see it as preaching mayhem, even though at times I found it equivocal concerning the treatment of the "people of the book" (Jews and Christians). But there was peace and harmony in our city, and friendly coexistence was the rule of the day. We used to visit Moslem, Jewish and Armenian friends, and they would return our visits. Many of them attended the same classes that we did. In our afternoons off we used to go together on picnics to Crusaders' castles by the Mediterranean coast or hike the beautiful mountains nearby. In those days there was no grudge against the Crusaders—over what they did and what they were alleged to have done—in the mind of our Moslem friends, nor any sign of mistreatment of the Jews in our neighborhood necessitating emigration to another nation.

Now as an adult, I often wonder where all the hate against each other and against the West has come from? I can understand their anger at Israel, a recent entity in their midst after 1948. But their hate of the West and of America is now exceedingly rampant. Has human nature changed that much? When President Roosevelt died on April 12, 1945, a few months before the end of World War II, all schools in the Middle East were closed the next day, and again the day of his internment. And all flags were flown at half-mast as a sign of respect for America, the country everyone loved. Today, when an American president dies his effigy is burned in the streets of the Middle East. What has taken place in a lapse of sixty years? How do we explain this great change in sentiment toward the United States between 1945 and 2007?

These questions must be discussed and answered in order to understand the reason for the venom being spouted all over the Middle East during the past half-century. An imbalance of power now permeates that area of the world, and opposing minds find themselves more inimical towards each other than they have been over many centuries.

Anything I say about either Israelis or Moslem Arabs, good or bad, is factual information which is not meant to belittle or antagonize one or the other. It is my hope that peace will eventually prevail between these two people of the book who had lived peacefully next to each other over many centuries, particularly, in Christian Spain before the *Reconquista* (1492). Their relationship then was amicable, indeed, even profitable, in both commerce and culture. When Moses Maimonides, the great medieval Jewish philosopher, found himself persecuted by his own people (because they considered his writings deviant from the Torah), he went to live in Arab Egypt, where he found peace and acceptance. He taught Arabic and Hebrew at Al Azhar University in Cairo for the rest of his life, and died in Cairo where he remains buried to this day. An oft repeated slogan in the West is that, "They've been fighting each other for years," meaning the Jews and the Arabs. That slogan is eminently false and shows an ignorance of history. In fact, from the beginning of the Islamic conquest in the seventh century A.D. to the end of the Middle Ages (1453), there was more harmony between Jews and Moslems than there were between either of them and the Christians.

I have many friends among both cultures, and it is my hope that some of the things I write do not displease one or the other. My quest is for truth and peace among them and between them and the West. I pray that peace among all people will reign again in the near future. But for that to happen they all must understand each other's hurts and needs, and thereby learn to live amicably with each other in this unnecessarily violent present-day world.

Dr. Hensley J. Hunter
April 3, 2007

Chapter 1

THE ABUSE OF TERMINOLOGY BY SPIN AND SLOGANS

The term "terrorism" began to be commonly used following the "régime de terreur" (1793-95) during the French Revolution (which began in 1789). Following those terrible years of the guillotine, the Revolutionary ideas of "liberté, fraternité, égalité" begun their slow spread throughout Europe, disseminated by Napoleon's armies. These ideas continue to influence us to this day and have, since 1989, entered even into what was formerly the Soviet Union. Of course there have been eras of terror throughout history. Alexander the Great's violent sweep through Syria, Mesopotamia and Persia created a reign of terror for these countries, until they were Hellenized (that is, accepted Greek culture).

Much later, the Northern barbarians, the Vikings and the Huns, created havoc and terrorized then Catholic Europe, while precipitating the fall of the great Roman Empire. Genghis Khan and Tamerlane (in the twelfth and fourteen centuries, respectively) created mayhem and terror by their lightning sweeps across Asia and Eastern Europe. I would think that much before all this took place, the Canaanites, the Amorites and the Jebusites met terror in the face when Joshua and his Hebrew tribes descended upon them, took over their land, and slaughtered every man, woman and child, as vividly reported in the Old Testament. The same terror can be seen in a painting I own, on the face of Priam, King of Troy, as he falls to the sword of Achilles, while in the background Troy is being swallowed by flames. So terror is as old as time itself. But the use and misuse of the term has been particularly common during the past few decades.

So what's in the word "terror?" Everything or nothing, depending on how that term is used. Words have been employed since time immemorial, alternately as means of communication or obfuscation. What did you do?" can mean either "Tell me what you did, I am sincerely interested in your actions," or, "How could you possibly have done such a horrible thing?" Or let us frame the question in two contemporary ways: The first being, "You, the suicide bomber, even though you did not succeed in performing your horrendous act, what could have possibly made you attempt such a horrible act? We would like to learn the basis of your mindset in order to try to moderate your actions, and possibly prevent such violence from taking place in the future." The second question would be entirely different, "You, the suicide bomber, you are an evil terrorist, belonging to Hamas, which we will put on our list of terrorist organizations. Further, we see no reasonable explanation that would mitigate your evil and horrendous attempt at killing yourself and your enemies, and we refuse to talk to you about why you did it."

A similar analysis could be carried out regarding plain, daily news reporting. To use a timely example, "Who started the July, 2006 war between Israel and Hezbollah?" The cause may be laid at the foot of Hezbollah because they crossed the blue border line between Southern Lebanon and Northern Israel and abducted two Israeli soldiers, while killing several others by attacking their tank with a rocket. Or could it be that after seeing an Israeli tank that had (in the first place) crossed the blue line towards Lebanon, Hezbollah chased it back across the border and then blasted it with one of their effective anti-tank rockets? Are we positive about the accuracy of either statement?

Cross-border misadventures by both sides had been taking place, on and off, for the previous six years. Furthermore, could the Hezbollah misadventure have been a sympathetic reaction on their part to the abduction of a dozen Palestinian cabinet ministers by Israel the previous week? And in turn, could those abductions have followed the abduction of an Israeli soldier in Gaza by jihadists the week before that? Furthermore, could the latter episode have followed the abduction of a Palestinian doctor and his brother the week prior to that? Or could it have been done in retaliation for the horrendous bombing by the Israeli defense forces (IDF) of two families of ten civilians each—who happened to be picnicking on a Gaza beach, on two separate days—another two weeks before that? The interconnection of all these events taken together cannot be ignored, as the American press had done, because that was, evidently, what started (and continued) the chain of events that produced these successive acts of violence.

So why did the media and all of our governmental agencies, all together with one voice blame Hezbollah for starting it all? Obfuscation is the applicable term for attributing the war's beginning—a war which devastated Lebanon, a third party in the standoff—to Hezbollah, while failing to mention the events of the previous four weeks. All our news media kept following the U.S. executive branch's constant repetitions in blaming the inopportune Hezbollah raid for being *the* cause of what ensued. Few analysts mentioned that the incident could have been in reaction to the chain of events that took place over the previous four weeks; or the possibility that the abduction of the two soldiers may have been used as a pretext by both Israel and the U.S. to start an invasion of Southern Lebanon, an operation reportedly planned a year before, with the purpose of destroying Hezbollah, the nemesis of both Israel and the Bush administration.

Let's look at another current slogan: "We will not talk to terrorists because this will show weakness on our part." Now, slogans may be simply catchwords ("terrorist," or "aggressor," or "axis of evil"); or they may be used because they are loaded phrases meant to produce a certain emotional response. Since when do we reserve talking only to our friends or to agencies who agree with us? Since time immemorial antagonists have acted in one of two ways. At first they would label as enemies the people they disagreed with, start a war against them, and proceed to kill them. Or, alternately, they would talk to them first to find out what their grievances were, and then would compromise and learn how to live with them. And if either or both of these methods failed to solve the impasse, the antagonists would snub each other and avoid dealing with one another for a while, until a new factor weighed in forcing them to change the status quo.

Israel normally starts by saying that they will not talk to abductors (and those they label as terrorists) while Hamas says they will not recognize Israel. But both sides invariably end up talking to each other, either directly or through intermediaries, and conclude by swapping a few of each other's prisoners. It's almost a face-saving charade. Worse yet, both Israel and the U.S. insist on not talking to adversarial governments, even though these had been democratically elected, at the insistence of both the U.S. and Israel—Arafat earlier, Hamas now.

The U.S. administration announces, "We will not talk to Iran. Their proposal falls quite short of our expectation." But since when do proposals give the opposing party everything they want? Or, we say, "they are running out of time" and we threaten them with invasion. How can time run out? Time has been going on since the foundation of the universe, and will continue till it ends. "Time is running out" was a slogan we kept repeating before we invaded Iraq. "We're running out of time" has become a slogan, a spin, a way of not compromising, perhaps a pretext to use our new armaments and see how they work in anticipation of a larger war.

Here's the most hypocritical of all slogans: "The Palestinians want to destroy Israel and throw it into the sea." How are they going to do that? By lobbing stones at Israel's F15s and F16s equipped with atomic warheads? Another slogan yet: "The Palestinians aren't prepared to talk." Since when do people occupied by a repressive regime refuse to talk about ending a cruel occupation? (It must be pointed out from the beginning that criticism of Israel's occupation of the West Bank and Gaza is not criticism of Israel's right to exist, which it is often made out to be.) The truth is that the Palestinians have been begging to talk to the Israelis for quite some time. Every time they are ready to talk, Mossad or Shin Bet assassinates one or two of their leaders. It is assumed that dead bodies can't talk. And, unfortunately, any time the Israelis want an excuse for a confrontation, the Palestinians unwisely oblige them: They send them suicide bombers or throw short-range rockets over the border. These moves accomplish nothing other than to bring Israel's fury on top of innocent Palestinians, the few by-standers not involved in the cross-border attacks who happen to be there—the culprits themselves having left the scene long before. It is collective punishment of a whole population, specifically forbidden by all Geneva Conference agreements. When the mouse plays with the cat, one knows who's going to eat who in the end.

The abuse of slogans and labels and the misuse of terminology have been practiced by adversaries throughout history. The examples above serve only to answer the questions, "What's in a word?" or "What's in a statement?" The prudent answer is that "statements" contain, either the whole truth, or part of the truth, or just plain falsehood. We are reminded of Plato's description of the Sophists of his time, using Socrates as his mouthpiece in the *Dialogues*. He accuses them of "making the better appear the worse, and the worse appear the better," depending on which side they represented. The Sophists were the advocates of social and political correctness, the opinion molders during that Periclean era of Greek history. Sophists were used as advocates by various parties to solve their disputes. They had no qualms about defending the guilty or accusing the innocent, "depending on which side paid them the better fee" (Plato). They were the movers and shakers in those days, just as their doubles today continue to make up the bulk of those claiming to be politically correct. Both then and now, sophists remain actively engaged in the creation of the spin and false slogans that move the emotions of the public at large in the direction they want them to move.

Oftentimes, spin and slogans are not perceived for what they are, a form of confusing, but subconscious, double-think. "I just want you to know that, when we talk about war, we're really talking about peace," said George W. Bush, in June, 2002. That statement could easily have appeared on a press release by the "Ministry of Truth" in George Orwell's satirical book, *1984*: "War is Peace and Peace is War!" Or it could have been straight out of his other great ironical parable, *Animal Farm*.

Fortunately, the use of falsehood often brings out honest people who stand up to defend the truth. These are individuals and institutions in our midst whose avowed function is to act as the devil's advocate, arguing against the accepted false slogans that they see bantered around repetitively in high places. These voices are still a minority crying out in the wilderness. Prominent examples are the editorial staffs of the Jerusalem newspaper Haaretz and of the Christian Science Monitor, who normally can be relied upon to advocate the painful truth. Tom Friedman, Robert Fisk, Pat Buchanan and others have spoken and written extensively about the abuse of slogans used to justify our stance, or Israel's, toward the Middle East crisis. Their views quite often contradict mainstream thinking. President Jimmy Carter's recent book, "Palestine, Peace or Apartheid," is a salient example of this. As of late, the former president has courageously embarked to defend its tenets on talk shows. Eighteen scholars, three of them Nobel Prize winners, have recently published remarks about the Middle East crisis in major newspapers across the globe:

> The latest chapter of the conflict between Israel and Palestine began when Israeli forces abducted two civilians, a doctor and his brother, from Gaza. An incident scarcely reported anywhere, except in the Turkish press. The following day the Palestinians took an Israeli soldier prisoner and proposed a negotiated exchange against the prisoners taken by the Israelis—there are approximately 10,000 Arab prisoners in Israeli jails. Typical of the double standards repeatedly employed by the West—and in face of what has befallen the Palestinians, on the land allotted to them by international agreements, during the last seventy years—is that this "kidnapping" was labeled outrageous, whereas the illegal military occupation of the West Bank and the systematic appropriation of its natural resources—most particularly that of water—is considered a regrettable but realistic fact of life. Today outrage follows outrage; makeshift missiles cross sophisticated ones. The latter usually find their targets situated where the disinherited and crowded poor live, waiting for what was once called Justice. Both categories of missiles rip bodies apart horribly—who but

field commanders can forget this for a moment? Each provocation and counter-provocation is contested and preached over. But the subsequent arguments, accusations and vows, all serve as a distraction in order to divert world attention from a long-term military, economic and geographic practice whose political aim is nothing less than the liquidation of the Palestinian nation. This has to be said loud and clear, for the practice, only half declared and often covert, is advancing fast these days, and, in our opinion, it must be unceasingly and eternally recognized for what it is and resisted . . . . (Signers included: John Berger, Noam Chomsky, Harold Pinter, Naomi Klein, Jose Saramago, Richard Falk, Gore Vidal, Arundhati Roy, Howard Zinn . . . . August, 2006)

There exist many Jewish Organizations in the U.S. and Israel (such as Brit Tzedek v'Shalom, Jewish Voice For Peace, Israel Policy Forum) who have opposed and indeed lobbied and fought against a one-sided American foreign policy, a practice undertaken to suit the advocates of a hard-line U.S. policy towards the Arabs and a more lenient one towards Israel. Here's the beginning of a letter sent to Secretary of State Condelizza Rice by Seymour D. Reich, president of the Israel Policy forum, on March 1, 2007:

On behalf of the Israel Policy Forum, we would like to commend your decision to join talks with Iran and Syria over the future of Iraq, and to push forward on the Middle East peace process. Like the recommendations of the Iraq Study Group, we believe that diplomatic engagement in the Middle East—even with unsavory regimes—is necessary to making political progress in Iraq and ensuring stability for our allies in the region.

The letter goes on to say:

We also support further consideration of the Arab League Initiative as a vehicle for restarting regional peace talks . . . Resolving the Arab-Israeli dispute is a critical component of reestablishing American influence and credibility in the Middle East. Talking and negotiations are the only way forward. That is why we can promise you our continued support for your diplomatic efforts.

Hopefully, a letter like this might help counteract the influence of the hawkish AIPAC (the American Israeli Political Action Committee) to stonewall any peace process. We can only wish there were similar voices in the Arab and Moslem world speaking against the ingrained and obstinate beliefs of their easily excitable populace. In that part of the world America is represented as Satan even when and where we are sending relief packages and monetary assistance to help their poor and disadvantaged.

To go against the grain is not always popular and seldom rewarding, but it is the correct moral behavior. It takes courage for these defenders of contrary views to speak against abuses in public policy, abuses that do not serve the best interests of the United States, or the long term interests of Israel.

Chapter 2

THE MACHIAVELLIAN WAY OF POLITICS AND GOVERNANCE

The practice of demonizing those we want to destroy is as old as time itself. Whether it is for the purpose of propagandizing the uninformed public, or whether it is due to internally motivated rationalizations in the mind of the accusers, rulers have commonly followed the Machiavellian way of hiding their unrevealed agendas under false claims of patriotism, and have led their public on crusades and wars that ended as disasters for their subjects. In times past, these misadventures often turned out to be sources of wealth and enlarged fiefdom for rulers and their favorites. Henry VIII was the Defender of the Catholic Faith against Lutheranism only a few years before he began demonizing the Pope and the Roman Church for not granting him a divorce. He then led his noblemen in the appropriation of the wealth of the monasteries, which, in due time, proved to be a disaster for the poor and disadvantaged people in England—that great number of small farmers who depended on the monasteries for work, education, charity and solace. Once the dukes and the lords of the realm appropriated all the wealth of the monasteries, they had no interest whatever in feeding or educating the poor who were previously fed, housed and educated at these now ransacked institutions. A great majority of King Henry's subjects were left destitute for centuries thereafter, a fact rarely mentioned in history books on the Reformation in England. There are hundreds of such examples throughout world history demonstrating how rulers and their entourage have obtained benefits from war and plunder, while leaving millions of the common people worse off than they were before the undertaking of the misadventure.

The invasion of Iraq in 2003 was preceded by much demonizing of Iraq's elite. Not that they were an innocent group, but the resulting condition of the common Iraqi at present is far worse than it was under the much publicized abuses that Saddam Hussein stands accused of having inflicted upon them. For a whole year prior to the invasion the American public was told repeatedly how Iraq had ignored seventeen U.N. resolutions, and that it had chemical weapons ready to be used against Israel. Yet, neither the administration nor the press ever mentioned to the public the fact that Israel for its part had ignored not only seventeen, but sixty-seven U.N. resolutions since 1967—a telling case of selective information. Nor did they ever mention the fact that Israel had hundreds of atomic warheads and tons of chemical weapons stored in silos underground. Would we have invaded Israel for possessing weapons of mass destruction, or for ignoring sixty-seven U.N. resolutions? And those are in addition to the thirty other resolutions against Israel that the U.S. had vetoed in the past forty years. When it comes to the U.N., the spin is frequently to blame that organization for being anti-Israeli. We often use selective information and withhold other related facts from the public, regardless of the merits or demerits of these U.N. resolutions against Israel.

For several years the public was inundated with information about Iraq's "weapons of mass destruction" and its ability and willingness to use them. If Iraq had any, none was used, and none was found following costly inspections and a costly invasion. With all the talk about WMD, the public was kept in total darkness about Israel's possession of two hundred atomic warheads and its arsenal of cluster and phosphorus-laced bombs (that we had given them). And there was not a single mention of that country's ability or willingness to use them, until July, 2,006 came around, when Israel used them by the thousands to devastate Lebanon's economy and to destroy its infrastructure, killing in the process over a thousand civilians.

At the time of the invasion of Iraq, Saddam Hussein was accused of having killed over 3,000 Kurds. Even though they may have been separatists in revolt against the central government (it is difficult to tell), Saddam's actions cannot be condoned. But what about the over 100,000 Iraqis said to have been killed in the 1991 war and the many more that have died so far in the present war (300,000 according to a John Hopkins University study)? Now we have a serious separatist civil war going on in Iraq—which Saddam Hussein had, in fact, kept from boiling over during his thirty-five-year of rule—not to mention the 3,300 innocent young Americans killed so far in the misadventure. Our claim to know what's good for the Iraqi people, better than what an Iraqi ruler would know, is a sign of arrogance. We are a nation two hundred years old claiming to know what's good for a four-thousand year old nation that has been the cradle of civilization.

The Machiavellian distortions, misrepresentations and accusations perpetrated before the invasion of Iraq were partially egged on by the national press and other news media, particularly, by the television crews of commentators and so-called military experts and retired generals. Most of them were of one voice with Rumsfeld and Cheney, not to mention Wolfowitz, Perle, Feith, Abrams, and Bolton. It is evident now that these people have derailed American foreign policy and contributed to President Bush's low approval rating, and consequently to his party's loss during the November 2006 election. Yet the President does not appear to have figured out the harm these people have caused him and the nation. He has yet to change his mind about the invasion or the need for it. Wolfowitz, called "architect of the war" by *Time Magazine*, was rewarded with the presidency of the World Bank.

On the CNBC afternoon stock market broadcasts, Lawrence Kudlow and Jim Cramer kept advocating on television the invasion of Iraq for a whole year, goading the administration to start the war. One could see on their faces (by their comments and their body language) their joy when President Bush decided to invade. Their talk show became more about Iraq and Saddam's evils than about stock market analysis, for which the program is intended. Fox News' archconservative Sean Hannity couldn't stop from advocating an immediate invasion of Iraq. These are but a few examples of the hysteria that pervaded the commentators on all main news channels before and during the invasion of Iraq.

Virtually, all the commentators, on all the networks, (except PBS's Jim Lehrer and Pacifica's Democracy Now), were supportive of the war. The warning voices of the few like Pat Buchanan, Jimmy Carter, or from the start the voice of the Pope, were barely heard in the tumult. There was widespread exuberance when our forces entered Baghdad unopposed. It did not occur to these "military experts" and commentators that perhaps Saddam Hussein, when he saw the inevitable, had ordered his Republican Guard to disperse and disappear as our forces got close to Baghdad. Or that he may have shrewdly suggested that they take only their light arms with them as they fled and to wait for a more propitious day to start an insurrection. We are seeing the results of that tactic now as we witness the insurgency's daily killing of our soldiers, and a fierce Iraqi civil war going on under our very eyes.

The governing elite are by nature self-serving. Nonetheless, humanity has yet to find an alternative method to replace government as a means for social survival. Governments are necessary, but the power inherent in them corrupts, and as Lord Acton once said, "absolute power corrupts absolutely." Besides, absolute rulers have always kept at their bedside Machiavelli's *The Prince*—a book which advocated for rulers an entirely different set of morals than the one they expect their subjects to follow. Nonetheless, there have been rulers who were attuned to their people's welfare, and who practiced the morals that their God expected of them. After all, virtue and morals were not an artificial creation; they have always been man's best natural endowment for survival and tranquility, both individually and collectively. "The life of virtue leads to the happiness that is every man's natural desire," wrote Aristotle around 350 B.C.

Louis IX, during France's thirteenth century, was canonized twenty-seven years after his death because he truly cared for the poor, the disadvantaged and the common man. He built the social services of his country and allowed neither the army, nor the nobility, to interfere with his social programs. Edward of England (St. Edward) governed wisely and compassionately. Stephen of Hungary (St. Stephen) was holy, virtuous and concerned with the welfare of his subjects. Henry II of Germany (d. A.D. 1024) was another saint who fought relentlessly for his people. He founded hospitals, schools, and churches throughout his realm. St. Ferdinand III of Castile did the same. All these monarchs lived and ruled during the thirteenth century, that "century of faith." Their lives show the falsehood of the oft heard belief that religion causes war.

In fact, it is secular rulers, those who believe in nothing higher than themselves, who foment the impiety of war. They follow Machiavelli, not the gospel. Such is the makeup of the false leaders who have ruled the world since human history began: The Ahabs, the Caligulas, the Neros, the Gengis Khans, and even crueler rulers like Robespierre, Hitler and Stalin. The worst evils of the 20th century were provoked by anti-religious, self-proclaimed atheists: Hitler, Stalin, Mao and Pol Pot.

Thank God that in our time, we have a preponderance of democratically-elected governments that are more attuned to their subjects' wishes; and yet, quite frequently, these wishes are manipulated and frustrated by greedy elected officials. Besides, we possess now extremely efficacious psychological methods often employed specifically as propaganda tools to manipulate the citizens' minds to conform to the ruling elite's agendas. How many citizens questioned their leaders' WMD theory that was used to invade Iraq? How many knowledgeable media commentators mentioned that Hezbollah was founded originally as a reaction to Israel's long-term occupation of Southern Lebanon (1982-2000)? How many people know or are ever educated about our fifty-year history of interference in Iran's internal affairs and in the structure of its government (see chapter 6)?

Thus governments find it useful (that is, pragmatic and convenient) to repeat in the ears of the public the slogans they invent. In fact, they repeat them so frequently that they begin to believe in them themselves. Rulers and regimes often become the victims of their own lies after constant repetition. We hear that, "We need a democratic Middle East, because in democracies people are less aggressive and do not subscribe to false ideologies." It has become the cornerstone of our Middle Eastern policy, and it would be wonderful if we could achieve it, considering the many advantages of such a form of government. But it doesn't necessarily lead to peace. The ideal of consumerism, encouraged within capitalistic democracies, has led, more often than not, to aggressive conquest and to the occupation of weaker countries that are rich in minerals and petroleum. That was the on-going relationship between France and Britain and their African and Asiatic colonies during the whole nineteenth century, the same era that saw the incipient rise and consolidation of democracies in the British Commonwealth and in France (during its Third Republic).

So what do slogans, spin, and the rest of political correctness mean? They signify very little to those who investigate their validity. Niccolo Machiavelli (1469-1527) advised rulers, in *The Prince* and in *The Art of War*, to use any means which achieves their end. He suggested the use of guile and secrecy to accomplish the ruler's hidden objectives and the use of the lie if it proves expedient to hide the governing body's real intentions. Some consider Machiavelli to have been the original utilitarian, the first pragmatist in politics. That is false. Long before him, the Sophists in Ancient Greece were proficient in the art of guile and manipulation. For the past 3,000 years these tactics have circumvented the will of many a nation's citizens and have lead to unnecessary wars, occupation and untold misery across the face of the earth.

Yet of all the historical slogans, the present term "terrorism" is the most inclusive generalization we have invented: It lumps all the people who disagree with us in one amorphous mass. Unfortunately, this makes it impossible to deal with them as separate entities, which is what is needed. Actually, terrorism rarely accomplishes its purpose. Gandhi accomplished more with his method of passive resistance than violent confrontation ever did. Even Yasser Arafat's initial use of terrorism—intended to bring the West to realize the original injustice perpetrated on the Palestinian people—did not accomplish his intended purpose. He wanted the world to become aware of the plight of the Palestinian refugees whose existence was being ignored by Israel and the West. He was readily labeled a terrorist by the West, and no lasting investigation took place into the cause of discontent among his people—an injustice that should have been dealt with at that early juncture of world terrorism. He ordered the high-jacking of airplanes and caused all sorts of mayhem, as if to say to the West: "We, the ignored Palestinians are still around. Do not forget us. We have a just cause." The West's blindness in refusing to acknowledge Arafat's intended purpose of liberating the Palestinians from Israeli occupation was the missed opportunity of the 1970s. Correcting that injustice could have nipped the spread of terrorism in the bud, before it spread into many other areas of the world. If the Israeli-Palestinian problem was settled with equal fairness to both sides right then and there, we would have probably avoided the interminable security lines at airports.

We must agree at this juncture that terrorist and violent behavior can never be condoned. It is immoral and ineffective. The end never justifies the use of evil means to achieve it. In Machiavellian politics this principle is ridiculed, and violence has been a part of history since the beginning of time. However, when violence occurs, it is essential to analyze the causes that led to it, and to see what corrections might be made to stop it or to prevent its recurrence in the future. Military confrontation should be the last step in the process.

It takes great wisdom, intuition and determination to discover and correct the causes of aggressive acts by the disadvantaged, by the militarily occupied and by poverty-stricken refugees. By acting more insightfully in the 1970s, we could have avoided several decades of violent aggression, including the great loss of American lives at the World trade center on 9/11, and the two Iraqi wars. Properly solving the Palestinians' tragic situation then could have saved many lost lives in Israel, the West Bank and Gaza, (indeed throughout the world,) and would have diminished the correlative number of widowed spouses, orphaned children and grieving parents.

However, there are different kinds of terrorist movements which appear to be nebulously-caused and authentically immoral and must be fought militarily. Even terrorism caused by a real injustice must not be condoned, but the injustice must be corrected. In any case, the recurrence of violent acts frequently fails to accomplish the intended purpose of the perpetrator, because the party being terrorized eventually becomes insensitive and loses compassion for the injustice the terrorist claims to have undergone. That is a normal reaction to recurring violence.

Chapter 3

EARLY HISTORY OF TERRORISM IN ISRAEL-PALESTINE

The Jewish Holocaust under Hitler, the massacre of Catholic Polish officers in the Katyn forest, the genocide of the Ukrainians by Stalin, the unbelievable atrocities of the Spanish Civil War, and the mayhem under Mao Tse-tung and Pol Pot—all these were incredible acts of terrorism performed by atheistic regimes or dictators ruling recognized nations. We normally reserve the term terrorism to signify acts done by individuals, but the greater extent of barbarism during the twentieth century was caused by powerful and atheistic states. Terrorist acts by individuals are limited in scope compared with state terrorism. Many of the terrorist acts carried on by individuals or by small groups are meant to bring attention to some injustice, considered trivial by some, but "patriotic" in the eyes of the terrorist. For centuries, people have labeled these acts as "terrorist" when performed by an individual or a group, but failed to stop the major terror of genocide when the massacres were carried on by a sovereign power under the guise of "state policy."

This twisting of nomenclature is now more evident than ever. Nations lay blame on the aberrant act of an individual rather than on their own. The frequent retaliatory acts in the Middle East and elsewhere—whether we call them individual or state terrorism—did not arise out of a vacuum. They have arisen out of a need to correct substantial grievances. In her book *Bring down the Walls,* Carole Dagher, research associate at the center for Muslim Christian Understanding, echoed this same point:

> A lot has been said and written about the repercussions of Zionism and the foundation of the State of Israel on Arab consciousness and on Islamic resurgence. Some developed the theory that it is precisely Israeli fundamentalism that has triggered Islamic fundamentalism. The establishment of the state of Israel in Palestine [1948] generated a powerful and virtually unending anti-Western sentiment. Since 1967, Israel has been increasingly identified with the West. And thus, the strains that characterize relations between the West and the Arab world owe a lot to the Palestinian tragedy. The unsolved Palestinian problem illustrates "the persecution, exploitation, oppression, and arrogance of Israel and the West towards the Arab and Islamic societies," to use the common Islamic lexicon.—Carole Dagher, *Bring Down the Walls*, p.38

According to Dagher, until the problem of Palestinian dislocation and suffering is resolved, Arab and Moslem grievances will continue, and we will not find the answer to what we call "terrorism." In fact, "terrorism" was the favorite tool used by Haganah, Irgun, and Lehi, the latter known to the British as the Stern Gang, in the establishment of the State of Israel. These were the names of the three most feared Jewish militias prior to, during, and following the events of 1948. All three groups created havoc in those days, before and during the establishment of a separate political entity in the midst of an already densely-populated Palestine. To understand one of the origins of present-day world terrorism, we must examine what took place in the Holy Land during the years before and after 1948.

There are references in the Bible to at least three dislocations of the Hebrew people. The first mentioned is their voluntary exile to Egypt from the time of Joseph son of Jacob to that of Moses (ca. 1700 to 1250 B.C.). The second was the forced Babylonian captivity in the sixth century B.C. And the third was the expulsion of the Hebrews from Judea by the Romans in 69 A.D. The biblical psalms written around the time of the Babylonian captivity illustrate the suffering and nostalgia of the Hebrews for what had become their adopted land (Abraham's covenant) west of the Jordan River. Psalm 79 eloquently narrates the longing of the Hebrews in exile:

> O God, the nations have invaded our land,
> They have profaned your holy temple.
> They have made Jerusalem a heap of ruins.
> They have handed over the bodies of your servants
> As food to feed the birds of heaven,
> And the flesh of your faithful

> To the beasts of the earth.
> They have poured out blood
> Like water in Jerusalem;
> No one is left to bury the dead.

It is nothing short of miraculous that two thousand and six hundred years after that psalm was written in Babylon, the Jewish people's exile ended with the establishment of the state of Israel, thus satisfying the longings expressed much earlier in Psalm 137:

> By the rivers of Babylon
> There we sat and wept, remembering Zion;
> On the poplars that grew there
> We hung up our harps.
> For it was there that they asked us,
> Our captors, for songs,
> Our oppressors, for joy.
> O how could we sing
> The song of the Lord on alien soil?
> If I forget you, Jerusalem,
> Let my right hand wither!
> O let my tongue cleave to my mouth
> If I remember you not,
> If I prize not Jerusalem above all my joys!

That longing while in Babylon was satisfied a mere eighty years later by the re-establishment of a Hebrew state. That state in turn lasted five hundred years until the final expulsion of the Hebrews by the Romans. But for the superbly poetic and deeply religious longing in Psalm 137 to be satisfied again in the twentieth century of Our Lord is the stuff that makes movies and legends. Yet the way it all came about is a less romantic story.

In 1897, the first Zionist Congress was held in Basel, Switzerland, led by Theodore Herzl. A declaration followed: "Zionism strives to create for the Jewish people a home in Palestine secured by public law. The Congress contemplates . . . the promotion on suitable lines of the colonization of Palestine by Jewish agricultural and industrial workers . . . The strengthening of Jewish national sentiment and consciousness, and preparatory steps towards obtaining the consent of governments where necessary [are needed] for the attainment of the aims of Zionism." Originally, "the northern frontier was to be the mountains facing Cappadocia (Turkey), the southern frontier the Suez Canal, and the Eastern frontier the Euphrates River in Iraq." This was the original and ambitious thought in Herzl's

Diaries. On October, 1899, David Trietsch wrote to Herzl, "I would suggest to you to come round in time to the 'Greater Palestine' program before it is too late."

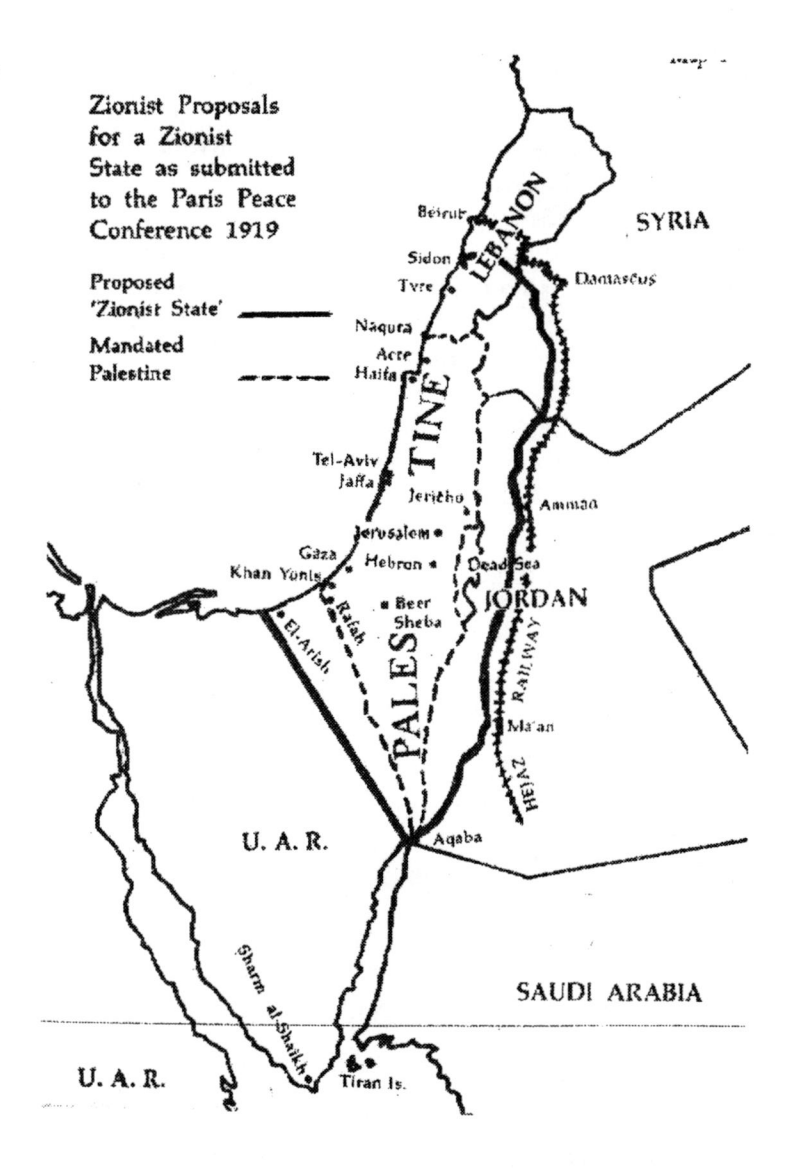

Modified Zionist Plan presented at the Paris Peace Conference, 1919, extending quite east of the Jordan River and encompassing South Lebanon including areas north of the Litani River.

On November 2, 1917, British Foreign Secretary Arthur Balfour issued his famous (or infamous) "Declaration" in a letter to Lord Rothschild, in which Britain, a first party, promised to give to a second party the land of a third party, even before it had possession of that land. Starting then, and four years before the mandate was granted by the League of Nations, the British government was fully committed to creating a national home for the Jewish people in Palestine. In 1919, the Zionist delegation to the Paris Peace Conference circulated a plan for a "Zionist State." It was a narrower vision than what Herzl had planned, but it called for unrestricted Jewish immigration and settlement in Palestine to be controlled by the Jewish Agency, a group formed to oversee the long-term Zionist project. It must be noted that was long before there was a Hitler and a Holocaust in Central Europe, a historical fact now conveniently used as a pretext for obtaining sympathy towards Israel's colonial policy (the settlements) dotting the West Bank and Gaza. At present, the illegal Israeli settlements in the West Bank are a natural follow-through on the original 1919 Zionist plan for the "Greater Israel."

All this was preceded by the machinations of the Sykes-Picot agreement between Britain and France in 1917, before the end of World War I, to allow them to rule Syria and Lebanon, Jordan and Palestine. Britain was given mandate over Palestine, covertly, to see to it that the Balfour declaration got implemented. This represented the injustice of one nation giving the land of a second nation to a third nation. Besides, all the promises of independence given by the British to the Arabs (through Lawrence of Arabia) to enlist them in the fight against the Ottomans were ignored. Lawrence himself, an honest man, felt betrayed by his own government and died ignominiously in 1935. All these manipulations were reminders of the splitting up of Poland, done in two successive steps, between Prussia's Frederick II, Austria's Maria Teresa and Russia's Catherine, two centuries earlier, when Poland disappeared altogether from the map. Poland as a country was later reestablished thanks to Napoleon, following his initial successes over Prussia and Austria, one of them being his great victory at the battle of Austerlitz, in 1806. The connivance of great powers over weaker ones is a sad part of history.

In 1917, when the mandate was promised, Palestine had a population of 700,000. Of these 644,000 were Arabs (574,000 Moslems and 70,000 Christians), and 56,000 Jews. In 1945, the total population had reached the figure of 1,784,000. Of these 1,230,000 were Arabs (1,020,000 Moslem and 210,000 Christians), and 554,000 Jews. Jewish immigration under the early British mandate became a deluge as the signs of European anti-Semitism were becoming more evident. Immediately after the start of the mandate, Britain allowed the Zionists to act as though they were a majority in Palestine. They became "a state within a state"—a reference used now regarding Hezbollah's presence in Lebanon. All the while Britain opposed any effort by the Palestinian majority towards self determination.

Needless to say, Palestinian Arab fears of a Zionist takeover began to be manifest throughout the country. The land being acquired by the Jews was becoming ex-territorial, meaning there were stringent rules placed on it after acquisition by the Jewish Agency. For example, a Jewish settler would be fined if he employed non-Jewish laborers, and once he owned the land he could never sell it back to an Arab. The acquired land became, as if to say, a trust of the Jewish Agency. Even though the Jewish population had reached twenty-seven percent by 1945, it actually owned only six percent of the land. Yet, on May 22, 1945, the Jewish Agency demanded the British to immediately establish the whole of Palestine "undivided and undiminished" as a Jewish state, to open immigration to all Jews who wanted to come, and to use international loans to fund such projects. And three years later the U.N. in effect gave fifty-six percent of the land to the Jewish settlers who three years before still owned no more than *six percent* of it. Is it a wonder that the Palestinians are still finding it hard, sixty years later, to swallow the injustice of that give-away that was imposed on them? If there is one thing that people will fight for, it is land, and particularly a forced land seizure of such proportions.

There were country-wide demonstrations, riots and strikes by the Palestinian Arab majority in 1920, 1921, 1929, and between 1936 and 1939. There occurred an Arab rebellion in 1936, in which the Palestinian leader of that time, the Grand Mufti Hadj Amin al-Husseini, butchered his Palestinian rivals. During the three years of the rebellion (called "the Events" in Zionist terminology) Palestinians killed more of each other than they killed of their British and Jewish opponents. Again, in the war of 1948, the Palestinians were split and splintered, lacking unified leadership and dependent on the mercies of the bickering Arab governments, who were intriguing against each other. They were unable to stand up to the much smaller, but organized Jewish community, which rapidly set up a unified and efficient army.

By 1946, Haganah, the Jewish military arm which was formed in 1920, had reached a force of 60,000, a full private army within the state. Two splinter groups arose from it, the Irgun Zvei Leumi and the Stern Gang, formed by more radical and terrorist-oriented elements. There were many acts of terrorism traced to these three groups. The most notorious was the blowing up of the King David Hotel on July 22, 1946, traced to Irgun, and causing the death of over one hundred government functionaries (British, Arab and Jewish). At that time one of those implicated was Yitzhak Shamir, who was to become Israel's prime minister, forty-five years later (1983). But as the partition of the country was being debated in the United Nations, the terrorist acts began in earnest, in the months prior to the sudden exit of the British (May 14, 1948), and before a single soldier from any Arab state had entered Palestine.

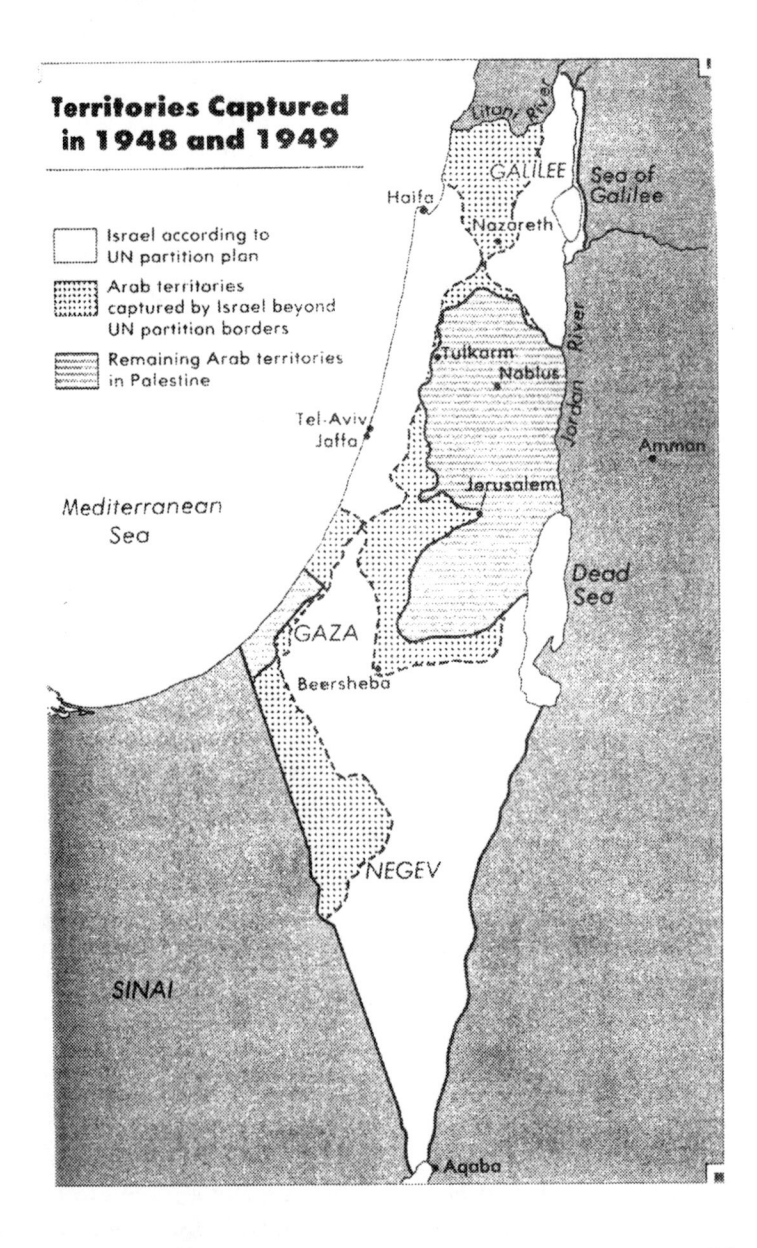

Territories outside the U.N. mandated border, captured by Israel in 1948 and 1949

Within the territory reserved by the U.N. for the "Arab state," the villages of Qastal, Saris, Qazaz, Salameh, and the towns of Jaffa and Acre, were attacked by the Jewish forces and annexed to the Israeli territory. Also within the territory of the future "Jewish state," the Arab inhabitants of Tiberias, Haifa, Safad, Beisan, (and a hundred other totally Arab villages) were attacked and the inhabitants massacred. Those who survived and refused to flee were expelled. The most infamous massacres of all occurred at Deir Yassin and later at Katamon (a predominantly Christian Arab neighborhood near Jerusalem) on April 9, and 29, 1948. The women and children were massacred first, and then the men were gunned down as they returned from their agricultural fields. Residents of Deir Yassin that survived the massacre were put on trucks and paraded through Jerusalem before they were shot. The purpose was to scare many poor farmers to flee their villages and take refuge somewhere else. It goes without saying that there was slaughter carried on by the other side also, but it was less organized and in line with the Palestinian Arabs' *Inshallah* (meaning literally, "If God wills," and figuratively, "leave it to God!")—they were not well prepared for that kind of fierce Zionist onslaught.

It was a month later (May 15, 1948) that the British occupying forces left Palestine and the Arab armies crossed the Jordan River to protect their fellow Palestinians' lives and rights, all to no avail. During the period of terror before the partition of the country, 400,000 Palestinian Arabs became refugees—that was in the six months before the involvement of the Arab states' armies (May 15); thus refuting the often-heard claim that the Refugees were told to flee by the advancing Arab armies—an old totally misleading spin. Eventually there were between 750,000 and 800,000 Palestinian refugees outside of Israel, while of the remaining Palestinians within Israel, about 100,000 became internal refugees within the state of Israel and have never been able to return to their original homes. Israel destroyed over 450 Palestinian villages to prevent any residents from returning. An even greater number of Palestinians became refugees during the succeeding wars of 1967, 1973, 1976, and the two Intifadas of 1987 and 2,000, respectively.

As to the claim that the Arab countries told the Palestinians to leave their homes, here is what Sir John Glubb, former governor of British Palestine, said:

> The story which Jewish publicity at first persuaded the world to accept, that the Arab refugees left voluntarily is not true. Voluntary emigrants do not leave their homes with only the clothes they stand in. They left in such a hurry that they lost members of their immediate family. The fact is that the majority left in panic

flight, to escape massacre. They were in fact helped on their way by occasional massacres here and there.—Glubb, *A Soldier with the Arabs*, p.251

Erich Fromm, the noted Jewish psychiatrist and philosopher, wrote:

> It is often said that the Arabs fled, that they left the country voluntarily, and that they therefore bear the responsibility for losing their property and their land, but in general international law, the principle holds true that no citizen loses his property or his rights of citizenship. The Arabs lost their property just because they fled? Since when, is that punishable by confiscation of property and by being barred from ever returning to the land on which a people's fore-fathers have lived for two thousand years?—Jewish Newsletter, New York, May 19, 1958

In recent years a number of Israeli historians, including Avi Shlaim and Benny Morris, have come to the same conclusion after gaining access to formerly secret official Israeli government documents.

On September 17, 1948, Count Bernadotte and his French aide, Colonel Serot, both United Nations emissaries, were assassinated in the Israeli part of Jerusalem to prevent them from concluding a peace agreement. The murders were committed by the Stern Gang whose leader was Yitzhak Shamir. Moshe Menuhin, the father of famed violinist Yehudi Menuhin, left Israel disappointed, and had this to say about the assassination:

> "Israel got away with murder. The U.N. demanded that Israel bring the assassins to justice; nothing happened. Count Bernadotte was the first martyr in the service of the United Nations' reconciliation efforts in Palestine—a saint to the Arabs and, as is usually the case, an anti-Semite in the eyes of the fanatical Israeli political nationalists. The sad part is that Count Bernadotte's plan was the reasonable answer to the Arab-Israeli conflict."—Moshe Menuhin, *the Decadence of Judaism in our Time*, Exposition Press, 1965, pp. 129,130).

Almost fifty years later, Israel's leader, Yitzhak Rabin was assiduously working for peace between Israel and the Arabs when he was assassinated, again by an Israeli extremist.

There are now over six million Israelis occupying a sliver of land along the Eastern Mediterranean Coast, and to even think of evicting them would be cruel and impossible. They are there to stay. For such people to fulfill their longing of two thousand years in such a way shows astonishing fortitude. But to persevere in an occupation over a weaker people by continuing to seize more of their land through illegal settlements, and by subjecting them to recurring humiliation and destruction, that is another matter.

Chapter 4

THE CONSPIRACY OF SILENCE AND THE RISE OF ARAFAT

Following the establishment of Israel in 1948—in a land that had not been designated as Israel for almost two thousand years prior to 1948—there was a conspiracy of silence dictating that the words "Palestine" or "Palestinians" are not to be used by any responsible publishing house, neither on maps, nor in books treating of the subject. Even though I held pro-Israeli sentiments at the time, I couldn't help but notice this avoidance in the West of the maligned term (Palestine or Palestinian) in what I saw or read in the media (radio, television, newspapers, magazines, or political essays) during those years. There was a tight blackout imposed.

After the 1967 Israeli military victory over the combined Arab Armies, the silence became even more pronounced. I continued to see no significant news-mention of Palestine or Palestinians. It was all about Israel and the *Arabs*. The Palestinians were about to become the forgotten race (like the American Indians) until Arafat assumed the chairmanship of the PLO (Palestine Liberation Organization). Previous to that, Arafat had been a successful civil engineer working in Kuwait, independently rich and well-settled. Shortly after his election, however, he began acts of terror to bring the world's attention to the Palestinians' plight.

Of course, things do change, and now there is a much greater awareness of the Palestinians existence, their suffering, poverty, isolation and Israel's iron-clad restrictions. M.J. Rosenberg of the Israel Policy Forum, a Washington-based liberal counterpart to AIPAC, wrote in *IPF Friday* last March (2006):

> Look, 25 years ago you couldn't even talk about the Palestinians. I mean, Golda Meir said there was no such thing as a Palestinian. Now there's not a single major Jewish organization except the far-right organizations that does not give at least nominal support to the two-state solution. So it's moving. It's kind of like the civil rights movement in this country. It's not perfect, but you see the change. I would say that 90 percent of American Jews understand that there's going to be a Palestinian state in the West Bank and Gaza, with East Jerusalem as its capital. That's what most Israelis know is going to be the future. So that's something.

Rosenberg's reference to what Golda Meir said is true. One recalls with total disbelief the Former Israeli Prime Minster, saying in 1969, "There is no such thing as a Palestinian people . . . It is not as if we came and threw them out and took their country. They didn't exist." That was said by Meir (The Sunday Times, June 15, 1969) in an effort to continue the fallacy of the original Zionist slogan: "A people without land for a land without people." There has been a definite improvement in recognition of the Palestinian cause, even if in nothing else, and the Palestinians have had to fight hard for it over the past forty years.

The PLO terrorist acts became prominent at the Olympic Games in Munich in 1972 when several Israeli athletes were taken hostage and later murdered, when the German authorities botched an attempt to rescue them. This episode was followed by several notorious high-jacking and rerouting of airplanes, all supposedly done to bring attention to the Palestinian problem. More violent incidents followed in which people lost their lives, and the use of terrorism slowly became symbolic of the various grievances of the Palestinians in the occupied area of former Palestine.

The Palestinian-Israeli problem should have been solved then, but, unfortunately, it was not. This point cannot be stressed enough. Every time the United States attempted a solution, either the powerful Jewish lobby in New York and Washington would derail it by obfuscation, or the Palestinians would refuse to accept in negotiations anything less than their total due. Instead, Israeli settlements began to be established in the occupied land against all Geneva Convention rules of occupation. Various U.N. resolutions *and* U.S. sanctions condemned what was overt Israeli colonization of Palestinian lands, but nothing more forceful was done about it. To this day, Israel has insisted that the Geneva Convention does not apply to the occupied territories and has refused to abide by it in the treatment of the occupied population.

Very few Americans asked why the Palestinians were engaged in terrorist activity, and no one seriously cared to apply pressure on Israel to stop the construction of settlements on occupied land, or to give up the occupation of the Palestinian areas (the West Bank and Gaza). Everyone talked about the terrorism, but few about its main cause. And when Israel destroyed the Lebanese civilian airline (Middle East Airline) in 1968, with its on-again-off-again bombardment of the Beirut airport, nobody called it state terrorism. Israel claimed that the Palestinians were using Beirut as their center to publish materials adverse to the Israeli state. But Lebanon has always been a land of refugees (Armenians, Poles, Greeks); and Beirut (along with Cairo) has always been the information and publishing center of the Arabic world. So it was not that unusual for the Palestinian Diaspora to be editing and publishing material in Beirut.

Several decades have elapsed without seriously taking into account the reasons for the terrorism within the Holy Land: At first, terrorism by the Jewish minority (1930-50), and later by the Palestinians (1970-2000). It is apparent to many observers at this stage that what was strictly a Palestinian tactic for obtaining recognition for their plight, has been adopted by every imaginable group all over the world as a cure for the world's ills and injustices. The situation is now out of control and the practice of the West and of Israel in using strong military action to solve these problems has aggravated the situation. It has produced more fertile grounds for volunteers to the cause of terrorism. Military responses have added fuel to the fire of grievances and injustices that should have been analyzed and resolved through peaceful means long ago.

At one time many Middle-East observers thought that the event of September 11, 2001, tragic as it was, would alert us to the world's fury against us. But the United States has ignored that monstrous warning signal of Islamic discontent. At first, because of world sympathy for us following the event of 9/11, we garnered the world's goodwill and its total support in our fight against al-Qaida. The exact opposite followed when we invaded Iraq without U.N. support, and without adequate consideration of the worldwide antipathy towards that war. We immediately alienated our European allies along with the rest of the non-aligned world.

Our latest attempts at manipulation in the Hezbollah-Israeli situation have not been in the least redeeming. In July, 2006, we procrastinated and delayed a cease fire, while Israel used our bombs to destroy the Lebanese economy and its infrastructure, at a loss of up to four billion U.S. Dollars: A very large amount for a small country.

Central Beirut, following Israeli bombardment for thirty three days, in July and August, 2006

Then we proceeded to offer Lebanon (at first) 30 million dollars towards reconstruction (less than one percent of the damage we helped cause by actively delaying a cease fire). To make things worse, we continued supplying Israel with our cluster bombs and phosphorus-laced rockets, which they continued dropping on Lebanon. Lebanon was our friend before and after the much-touted Cedar Revolt of 2005. But it seems that we know how to lose a friend and turn him into an enemy. What I hear now is that the Maronites in Northern and Central Lebanon, who for sixty years have been sympathetic to Israel, have become dead set against it ever since the events of July, 2006. Unfortunately for us, the Arab world is quite aware that we reward Israel's occupation and settlement of Palestinian land with over three billion dollars a year in aid, excluding military giveaways, and we have persisted in doing it annually for the past half-century, regardless of the damage to our name that Israel foments when it behaves like a bull in the delicate Middle Eastern china shop.

Terrorism will be stopped by paying attention to the reasons it exists. It is true that some of these reasons can be rationalizations on the part of terrorists. But most of them are not, and should be properly addressed. Pope John Paul II had said many times, "If you want to work for peace and end terrorism, you must work for justice and practice it in the world."

Chapter 5

THE WIDESPREAD PRESENCE OF TERRORISM IN OUR TIME

Terrorist activity has surged in various unconnected regions of the world. The Israeli-Palestinian problem was the foremost cause of terrorist acts in the 1940s, and later in the 1970s and 80s. It could have been resolved long time ago, for it was a straight-forward problem: The Palestinians wanted the removal of Israel's armed forces of occupation from those territories which are part of the lands the United Nations assigned to them in 1947. Furthermore, they have been asking to be recognized as a national entity by all nations, for quite some time to no avail. (Again it is necessary to repeat that criticism of the occupation of the West Bank and Gaza does not mean denying Israel's right to exist.) Early on, the objection of the Palestinians was the very presence of the State of Israel. Things have changed and the great majority of Palestinian Arabs now accept the idea of two states living side by side. The Palestinian have even accepted to have a state of their own that is merely twenty-two percent of the former Palestine, even though the U.N. had originally given them forty-four percent.

In essence, the Palestinians have been saying: "Israel! Get out of the Palestinian areas of the West Bank and Gaza and take out your intrusive settlements with you, and then there will be no reason for the existence of any Palestinian liberation (called terrorist by you) organizations, or any reason left for us not to recognize your right to exist!" Of course, the Palestinians' dilemma in recognizing Israel has been all along: "Which Israel are we being asked by the West to recognize: The original 1948

U.N. creation? The post-1967 enlarged Israel? The Greater Israel with the 400,000 settlers and settlements dotting every area of our countryside? We repeat: Which Israel is the Western World expecting us to recognize? Which part of Israel's continuously expanding borders are we to accept? Are we to recognize even the stolen and sequestrated areas now being enclosed within the boundaries of the monstrous Sharon wall that is being built exclusively on our land?"

No one in the U.S., or within the Israeli administration, or in the news media, has the courage to talk about Israeli occupation as being one reason for the so-called Palestinian problem in recognizing Israel and the ensuing terrorism. We ask ourselves, why is that so? Many observers point the finger at the powerful pressure the Jewish lobby exerts in the U.S., particularly, the influence of the American Israeli Political Action Committee (AIPAC), a group connected with a select number of other Jewish American Organizations, most of them catering to the prosperous and influential Jewish voices in New York and Washington. These groups are always doing the bidding of the more hawkish parties in Israel—even though a sizeable number of American Jews are not in sympathy with that hard-line stance and see it as a hindrance to any permanent state of peace and tranquility for Israel. Liberal Jewish observers—and most Jews are fairly liberal—point to the fact that the number of American Jews supporting AIPAC is quite small. They say that the majority of young Jews in America are actually as indifferent to the Middle East problem as is the average American who pays little or no attention to it.

The unchallenged motto of the groups supporting the hawkish stand of AIPAC is, "What's good for Israel is also good for the United States." This is an invalid and dangerous assumption since the interests of both countries are not the same. That attitude has played a great part toward our loss of influence in the Arab and Moslem world, and even among our European allies. There is a universal loss of confidence in our ability to act as honest brokers in solving a problem that only the U.S. can solve—because we hold the strings of annual military and economic aid to Israel. One administration after another would work on and off on a solution, only to see their work derailed by Jewish-American lobbying. It is well known that both U.S. political parties compete with each other in catering to the lobbying Jewish-American organizations for donations at election time.

If Israel were to withdraw from the occupied Palestinian lands (as they legally and morally should), would certain groups of Palestinians still talk about the destruction of Israel? Most experts doubt that they would. Withdrawal of forces would pacify the situation, goodwill will ensue, and all talk (even by splinter and non-consequential Palestinian groups) of

Israel's destruction would stop, being in any case the ridiculous gibberish it is. No one seriously believes that the Palestinians, using stones and pebbles as armaments, can destroy the premier military power in the entire Mediterranean basin. Besides, the "throwing-Israel-into-the-sea" motto—even when first pronounced by Gamal Abdul Nasser in 1967—was nothing more than Arab hyperbole. Yet the news media keep repeating that slogan, even while it is evident that it is Israel who keeps encroaching more and more into the Palestinian territories with iron-clad occupation and new settlements. In fact, what the entire world sees now is that Israel has been gradually "pushing the Palestinians towards the Jordanian desert," rather than "the Palestinians pushing Israel into the sea." And that is precisely why many observers now believe that even the idea of a separate Palestinian state may no longer be feasible. There are too many Jewish settlements and restricted military roads crisscrossing the area originally assigned to the Palestinians. It has become a split-up, ungovernable Bantustan in every respect. (Bantustan is the term given to isolated, non-contiguous land.) That was one reason why Arafat couldn't possibly accept at Camp David a proposed Palestinian state that had no contiguity of territory and no outlined borders.

President Carter states all that clearly in his new book (*Palestine, Peace or Apartheid*, Simon and Schuster, 2006). According to the President, the general parameters of a long-term, two-state agreement are well known. He postulates that there will be no substantive and permanent peace for any of the peoples in this troubled region as long as Israel is violating key U.N. resolutions, official American policy, and the international "road map" for peace by occupying Arab lands and oppressing the Palestinians. He emphasizes that except for mutually agreeable negotiated modifications, Israel's official pre-1967 borders must be honored. And he emphasizes, furthermore, that as with all previous administrations since the founding of Israel, present U.S. government leaders must be in the forefront of achieving the long-delayed goal of a just agreement that both sides can honor.

Now, for a better understanding of the rise and proliferation of the various so called "terrorist" movements that have arisen across the world, let us turn to these various organizations, one by one.

a. The Palestine Liberation Organization. In the late 1960s and early 1970s, the rise of the PLO was a predictable natural occurrence. The Palestinian cause was being ignored. In fact, what appeared to be a conspiracy to forget them was taking place. So the PLO was formed and eventually Yasser Arafat became its head. For a few years the PLO's violent actions across the globe seemed "successful" in the sense of having exposed the world to the just demands of the Palestinians and to their plight as dispossessed refugees. Once they made their point by making their existence known, they began to reduce the violence, ultimately foreswearing it altogether and accepting Israel's right to exist. Galling to them as it is, they have had to accept as *fait accompli* what they still call the disaster (the *nakbeh*) of 1948. In a way, they have had to swallow their Arab pride, and go along with the American and Israeli interests and wishes. But the problem is that up to now they have gotten very little for their forthright acquiescence.

Arafat was marginalized. No one on the American or Israeli side would talk to him, imprisoned as he was on one acre of land in his own country, and constantly harassed by the IDF (Israeli Defense Forces). He had forcibly become a dead end zero for all his work for the liberation of the Palestinian people and their land. With his downfall, new movements arose and became more violent. Most Palestinians thought of the new kids on the block (Hamas and others) as better able to represent their aspirations and interests, and in an attempt to replace the de-fanged PLO—which by then had been mercifully taken off the U.S. terrorist list—they democratically voted in Hamas. How could they forget Hamas' diligent help in education, social work, and promptness in helping them rebuild their homes once destroyed by the occupying Israeli soldiers? And that, provided they can obtain a building permit from their Israeli overseers, a task like asking them to part the Red Sea.

b. Hamas came into being as an offshoot of the Muslim Brethren in the late 1970s. Israel actually assisted Ahmad Yassin, the leader of the Brotherhood, in creating Hamas in the Palestinian territories as an opposing force to Arafat and the PLO. Robert Dreyfuss in the *Devil's Game* believes the same: "Israel started Hamas," he writes. Charles Freeman, the veteran U. S. diplomat and former ambassador to Saudi Arabia agrees: "Hamas was a project of Shin Bet (the Israeli domestic intelligence agency) which had a feeling at the time that they could use it to hem in the PLO." Hamas first grew slowly, but later came into prominence because of the void created both by the marginalizing of the PLO, and by the bankruptcy of the Palestinian economy.

In the late 1990s Hamas grew into a terrorist group that killed many Israelis. The second Intifada started in 2000, following the aggressive show-of-power entrance of Sharon (and his strongmen) into the Dome of the Rock, the Palestinian religious compound. Suicide bombers—not to be condoned—proliferated as one means of resistance from a people who had nothing but their bodies to resist with. They were methodically put down by Sharon's resolve and strong-arm tactics. He entered their and their refugee camps, uprooted their trees, and destroyed their homes and their will to resist. The worst damage occurred when the Israelis destroyed all the computers in the Palestinian authority offices in Ramallah, thus eliminating all vital records of Palestinian lives and land ownership. It was one way of turning the Palestinians into non-beings. On the other side, suicide bombing was becoming a weekly occurrence within Israel, an intolerable situation.

What about the suicide bombing? It was a practice that ultimately proved unsuccessful and was generally abandoned four years later as it failed to accomplish any positive results for Hamas. Unfortunately, it has re-surfaced with a vengeance in Iraq as a means of showing opposition to the presence of the occupying American and British forces. Violence cannot be condoned, but it is not difficult to see it rise in areas of dire poverty, despair and hopelessness. The oldest recorded incident of a suicide bomber was the case of the Hebrew Samson, blind, shackled and despairing, pushing apart two supporting columns of the temple of Dagon, the god of the *Philistines* (the Semitic word for Palestinians), during a religious service, thus collapsing the temple and killing himself along with hundreds of religious observers. That case of suicide-bombing has been celebrated by our parents and grandparents for over three millennia as an example of courage, a heroic act.

Over time, Hamas began to be more concerned with the basic needs of the Palestinians than the PLO ever had. One of the objections to the PLO by both the U.S. and the world community had been the graft and fiscal irresponsibility under their tenure. The same cannot be said of Hamas. They are intimately involved in the social service of their constituents—in building and running schools and hospitals, in feeding the poor, and in emergency services and support. (Hezbollah has done the same for the poor Shiites in Southern Lebanon.) As of late, Hamas' candidates have won a majority of seats in the Palestinian Parliament through a democratically run election monitored by American and European observers, including the perennial watcher, Jimmy Carter.

The present Israeli leadership keeps saying, "We don't have a peace partner to talk to," while they continue assassinating the Palestinian leaders they could talk to. President Bush had asked for democratic elections in Palestine, in view of his stated goal of building democracies in the Middle East. And yet when these democratic elections produced a party that was not to his liking (or Israel's), he refused to accept the result, and refused to talk to the elected leaders.

We have not been honest in our dealings with the Palestinians. It is most surprising that they still want us as brokers in their dispute with Israel. Over the past fifty years we have sent to the Middle East many emissaries to act as arbitrageurs between the Palestinians and the Israelis. Oftentimes, the emissaries selected were American Jews, some of them having had previous association with AIPAC. Starting with Kissinger down to Dennis Ross, we have kept that practice alive, knowing full well that the eyes of the Arab world are focused on this anomaly.

The U.S. must cease using the terrorist label and start talking to both the PLO and Hamas, both having been elected by the Palestinians as their spokesmen. And we must stop waiting selectively for a Palestinian regime that would do our bidding. Before the partition of their land, the Palestinians, along with the Lebanese, were the most progressive people in the Middle East. Many of them were educated professionals who had studied in European and American Universities. Their civilization has been utterly crushed by the foot-dragging of the West and by Israel's desire for more land. True, there are still other more fanatical organizations among the radical Palestinians, such as Holy Jihad or Al Aqsa Martyr's Brigade, who may continue preaching the destruction of Israel, even if peace comes around—although I believe their voices will be of no consequence once the majority of their fellow Palestinians are living in a non-occupied state of their own. By then the main cause for the fury of the extremists would have ceased to exist.

In a recent communication, Uri Avnery, an astute observer, proclaimed that "If Hamas did not exist, it would have had to be invented. And if a Palestinian government is set up without Hamas, we should have to boycott it until Hamas was included. And if negotiations do lead to a historical settlement with the Palestinian leadership, we should make it a condition that Hamas, too, must sign it." His view is that Hamas represents at least fifty percent of the Palestinian people, and there is no sense leaving such a large group out of a peace accord. It would continue to fight against a settlement that did not include it.

Fortunately, a unity government has just been formed between Fatah, Hamas, and three other splinter groups. It was signed in Mecca on March 17, 2007. This was done through the auspices of the Saudi Arabian King, who was most assuredly pushed into brokering this deal by his friends in the Bush administration. This is great news, as the Saudis and the other Arab states have already outlined the parameters of the Taif accord of 2002, a peace proposal which calls for diplomatic relations and recognition of Israel by all Arab countries, provided the latter withdraws to its 1967 borders and accepts the establishment of an independent Palestinian state. It is the one proposal that has survived as an acceptable option, now that the so-called "Road Map to Peace" has gone nowhere. This new "Mecca Agreement," signed by the various Palestinian factions, was also approved by the Arab League on March 29, 2007.

c. **Hezbollah** is an armed Shiite movement which arose during the 1982-2000 long Israeli occupation of Southern Lebanon. This movement of Southern Lebanese Shiites was a natural reaction to Sharon's Israeli military invasion of 1982, which in the end proved inimical to the best interests of both Israel and Lebanon. Hezbollah is listed as a "fanatical" Shiite organization, supported by Iran. Yet it seems no more fanatical or hawkish than that minority of hard-line Israeli leaders and their evangelical Christian supporters, who are advocating the aggrandizement of Israel through forcing the Palestinians out of their remaining small piece of land. Hezbollah demonstrated its legitimacy during the latest 2006 Israeli invasion, by proving itself as the dogged defender of Southern Lebanon, even in the eyes of their Christian Lebanese enemies. And now, they have taken the lead in providing the social services needed in the reconstruction of the devastated nation.

Hezbollah has become a political, social, and military force in Lebanon. It is difficult to be a great lover of Hezbollah's fanatical Shiite predisposition. Their Moslem fundamentalism has not endeared them to the Sunni and Christian constituencies in the North of Lebanon. Yet, they are in fact Southern Lebanese who get their arms from Syria and Iran, a situation little different than the role the U.S. provides in the supply of phantom jets, missiles and cluster bombs to Israel. Arabs in the larger Middle East are siding with Hezbollah's position and feel that what's good for the goose is good for the gander—meaning that the ballyhoo in the American media about Iran supplying Hezbollah with arms is true, but so is the U.S.'s unceasing supply of the latest strategic armaments to Israel. They say that Hezbollah's closeness to Syria or Iran is a fairly recent reaction to decades of the U.S. plying Israel with jets, tanks, bombs, and rockets. And in all fairness, it may be further argued that Syria and Iran are at least acting within their regional sphere of influence (just as we do in our embargo of Cuba), whereas the U.S. is reaching out ten-thousand miles to meddle in the affairs of nations. Zbigniew Brzezinski, an influential foreign policy analyst in Washington and former security adviser to President Carter, agrees with this assessment.

Brzezinski was outspoken during the 2006 Lebanon conflict, calling Israel's response to Hezbollah's attacks "dogged, heavy-handed, politically counter-productive and morally unjustifiable." He remarked, "When we supply Israel with cluster bombs, that's supposed to be an act of international friendship and peace; but when Iran supplies the Palestinians or Hezbollah with a weapon, that means terror." Those remarks were made last year at a dinner hosted by the New America Foundation. He added, "Bush should say either, 'I make policy on the Middle East' or 'AIPAC does'."

Zbigniew Brzezinski has just come out with a new book titled *Second Chance*. He was interviewed about it on PBS nightly news the evening before my text was sent to the publisher. During the half-hour interview Brzezinski discussed the same problems covered here in *Terrorism or Patriotism*, almost chapter by chapter. It is understandable that Brzezinski and many other observers are worried about the same concrete problems treated in this present book—all of them arising from our skewed Middle East policy. But of more interest here, is how Brzezinski graded the last three American presidents on their handling of diplomacy and foreign policy during their terms in office: "From the competent but conventional thinking of the first Bush administration, to the well-intentioned self-indulgence of the Clinton administration, to the mortgaging of America's future by the 'suicidal statecraft' of the administration of the second Bush," he said in the interview.

Brzezinski gave Bush Senior a firm B. Of course, Jim Baker was his secretary of state, and that must have helped him get that grade. He gave Clinton a D, and thought that Clinton missed a golden opportunity to solve the Middle East problem when he had a chance to do it under his tenure. But he gave G.W. Bush, Jr. a resounding F for having antagonized the entire world by "misreading the sign of the times." Brzezinski talked about how, "G.W. Bush, during all six years of his presidency so far, has acted as if he was still living in the colonial times of a century ago." He called his administration "catastrophic," blaming him for having been unaware that the world is in "a decidedly post-colonial era now." He also faulted him for having surrounded himself with and given power to several officials (the pro-Israeli neo-cons) who had had only minor roles under Bush Senior and Clinton. Brzezinski stated that their advice to the President has been detrimental to the best interests of U.S. foreign policy.

As for Hezbollah, it must be taken for what it is, a fundamentalist Southern Lebanese entity that liberated South Lebanon from Israeli occupation several years ago, and with help from Syria and Iran has defended Lebanon again in the recent war (July, 2006). It is also providing essential social services in Southern Lebanon and helping in the reconstruction. It should eventually be disarmed, but not until Israel signs a peace treaty with Lebanon, and hopefully, accepts the formation of a Palestine for the Palestinians. If Hezbollah is disarmed, who would stop the Israeli army next time around from going all the way to Beirut if they thought it served their purpose?

Lebanon has never invaded and occupied Israel, nor could it ever do so. This small country prides itself on being like Costa Rica or Denmark, a country with more teachers and professionals than soldiers. It is a peace-loving country. Even its enemies admit that. As long as a Lebanese is practicing his talent as a successful doctor, lawyer, teacher or middleman in business, he is content. He has never been warlike throughout history. Lebanon has been conquered and occupied many times over the centuries, but it has never conquered others, except perhaps through trade and commerce. That's how the Lebanese (and their predecessors, the Phoenicians) have won over their conquerors in the past. That's also one of the reasons why Lebanese Americans, unlike their Jewish neighbors, rarely use political pressure or get involved in lobbying for Lebanon's, or any other, cause within their country of adoption. Sanford Holst in his book, *Phoenicians, Lebanon's Epic Heritage*, mentions religious tolerance, peaceful resolution of conflicts, social adaptation, and international trade as the hallmarks of the Phoenician-Lebanese genetic makeup.

It must be admitted that there exist many other organizations still using senseless, violent and destructive means of terror, while Hezbollah and Hamas have calmed down considerably as of late, and have begun to use non-violent means of contact and dialogue. We must encourage them in that behavior, instead of continuing to antagonize them by keeping them on the infamous "terrorist list." The atrocity they committed against the Marines in Beirut in 1983, difficult to forget and tragic as it was, must be forgotten, just as we have had to put aside our Vietnam atrocities as part of the past. We have our hands full at present with the insurgency going on in Iraq, where car-bombings, wanton executions and all sorts of violence are daily occurrences. To equate Hezbollah with al-Qaida or with the Sunni-Shiite explosion in Iraq would be somewhat misleading.

Hezbollah is not unreasonable in its refusal to disarm until the frequent and disproportionate military reactions from the Israeli side show more balance. And there seems to be no change in that Israeli *modus operandi* as of yet. In the meantime, both Hezbollah and Hamas should be taken off the terrorist list, and dealt with by dialogue. This may give us a much needed insight into Iran and Syria as well. That is how enemies are turned into friends, and possibly into supporters (and even collaborators) in our cause to democratize the Middle East. After all, Hezbollah has already entered the political process in Lebanon, and succeeded in doing so by fair and democratic elections. Hamas was equally chosen in a well-monitored democratic election to represent the Palestinian people. Do we or don't we want a democratic Middle East?

d. Al-Qaida's story is well known by now. Osama bin-Laden's break with his own very rich, capitalistic Saudi family is part of Middle Eastern lore. He gave up a bright future as entrepreneur and money-maker for a cause that he believed in—even though it is a cause condemned by the entire civilized world. Unfortunately for bin-Laden, all his mayhem has resulted in no lasting solution to the problems of the region, and has alienated the world from his cause. He first fought along with the Taliban, and with American support helped remove the Russian presence from Afghanistan. Then he joined forces with the Taliban's restrictive mullahs, supposedly feeling alienated by America's immodest way of life (in his words). At that time he was also very incensed at the establishment of U.S. military bases in Saudi Arabia, which he considered sacrilegious. The result was the eventual attack on the Twin Towers in Manhattan on September 11, 2001. That violent act was a very tragic incident that infuriated us along with the whole world. We had the entire world's sympathy when we invaded Afghanistan, and that war is still in progress. Then we antagonized the entire world by our invasion of Iraq, and we are still mired in Afghanistan, fighting a new generation of Taliban.

The problem with al-Qaida is that its resentment of the West is based on philosophic and religious differences, both abstract and difficult reasons to deal with. It is an enmity that is difficult to resolve, other than through constant military containment. We can only isolate and destroy the tentacles of the movement, while at the same time lessening their ability to recruit discontented young fighters by speedily embarking on a solution to the Palestinian problem. We could also pay more attention to the moral image we project to the world—an image that al-Qaida's adherents love to proclaim daily to the rest of the Moslem world. It is, in fact, an image that could undergo a little cleansing.

e. The Iraqi insurrection. That is a problem that we helped create when we opened a vipers' nest by invading Iraq and toppling Saddam Hussein. We were presumptuous in thinking that we could manage the centuries-old rift between Sunnis, Shiites and Kurds better than an indigenous leader could have, and in fact had done. So we got rid of the dictatorial leader and opened a can of worms. One cannot help but smile at our naiveté when we complained about the strong and cruel, yet difficult, measures he undertook during his thirty five years in power to contain the Sunni-Shiite-Kurdish problem and keep his country together. It is a task that we have been unable to accomplish for one single month since we've been there. How tragic has been the advice given to President Bush by the neo-cons, who had infiltrated and taken over the White House, the State Department and the Pentagon. And this coupled with the spineless acquiescence of Congress when they voted to let the president decide what to do. This war will go down in history as one of the most shameless episodes in U.S. foreign policy.

There is no need belaboring the issue of whether the war was justified or not. Especially, when there was universal disagreement from the very start with our position vis-à-vis Iraq. There were repeated warnings not to enter this war from France, Russia, China, the U.N., the Pope, the Archbishop of Canterbury, the Arab League, and all other voices of reason and prudence. Yet an unholy alliance developed between rabid neo-cons and Israel's promoters within the U.S. (most of whom are these same neo-cons), along with the tacit support of Cheney and Rumsfeld, and the Christian Zionists. They had all infiltrated their way into President Bush's confidence, roused up the American public by spin and slogans, and thus succeeded in pushing the United States into a questionable war. Their success was short-lived now that Iraq is in the grip of terrorists of the worst kind. That poor country has been ripped apart beyond description. Is Iran the next target of that same unholy alliance of neo-cons and Christian Zionists? Is Iran the only Middle Eastern country still left that can stand up to Israel's military dominance in the region? If so, the cry will be to unbalance Iran like we have surely done to Iraq, the one country which could have stood up to Iran, our present nemesis.

f. Arab and Moslem nationalism were spurred on initially by Great Britain's betrayal of the promises of independence it had made to the Arabs for the help they gave it in defeating the Ottoman Turkish Empire during the First World War. Recall the Lawrence of Arabia story and his efforts after the war to remind Britain of those promises. With that betrayal and the subsequent establishment of Israel, the Arabs, who had been asleep since their days of glory 800 years before, suddenly woke up to the fact of the West's betrayal, and began to dwell on what they considered the confiscation of Arab land in Palestine without their approval or consent.

Nothing wakes up sleeping giants as rapidly as the introduction of a foreign irritant into their body politic. The great British historian of the past century, Arnold Toynbee, studied twenty-two civilizations in his ten-volume *Study of History*. He outlined how the awakening of a strong religious zeal in a culture, coupled with that civilization's encounter with a worthy antagonist, invariably causes a dormant civilization to rise to a golden age. We did that with the Arabs at the precise time when they were beginning to stir with religious fervor and nationalistic zeal. We introduced in their body politic, a new antagonist, Israel, which became their irritant, a "foreign body" they found difficult to digest. With increased revenues from petroleum and other raw materials, their economic strength was beginning to improve. They were satisfied at that time with selling us oil at two dollars a barrel—until we awakened them through our unfair and one-sided support of the same foreign body we introduced in their region. Presently, oil has reached the price of sixty to seventy dollars a barrel, a much higher price than we had been paying for it, even with due adjustment for inflation.

Other mishaps of our foreign policy in the area followed in due course. In the 1973 Egyptian-Israeli war, when it was announced that the U.S. had just rushed a large number of fighter planes and state-of-the-art tanks to Israel, several observers predicted that the Arabs would start an oil embargo, since that was their only weapon. Shortly after, the oil embargo began in earnest. The lines at the gas pumps in the 1970s marked the beginning of our sudden realization of our dependence on Arab oil. That, in turn, alerted them to our addiction to oil, and to our willingness to pay any price for the black gold which is the driving engine of our economy.

In 1973, Egypt was actually trying to recover its land, the Sinai Peninsula, from Israeli occupation. Anwar Sadat was then Egypt's president; and as later history was to prove, he was a moderate leader who ultimately signed a peace agreement with Israel. So, why did we take sides in that 1973 war to our own detriment? Because we wanted to police the world and we thought that through a strong Israel we might control the Middle East. We have continued to operate on that false assumption ever since, up to and including our misguided invasion of Iraq. We have failed in that policy and half of the world no longer respects us because of it. We don't seem to realize that in all of our other endeavors we are envied by the entire world, from our scientific innovations, to our workable economics, to our high standard of living—*until* we play Machiavelli and attempt to control the rest of the world.

g. Chechnian and Kurdish Nationalism. These two liberation movements (along with other similar movements) are examples of long-festering sores that can be resolved. They both represent patriotic national ambitions using terrorist tactics to achieve their independence. They fall into the same category as Hamas and the PLO, and possibly Hezbollah. These are Moslem people with national aspirations, just as the Armenians, for example, had national aspirations for years until an Armenian state was finally created at the time of the fall of the Soviet empire in 1990. An example of how these problems can be resolved is the creation of East Timur. It was formed several years ago as a separate entity from Indonesia, to accommodate the Catholic population of that region who prior to their independence suffered constant harassment and persecution at the hands of the Indonesian Moslem majority.

The Russians look upon the Chechnians as terrorists, just as the Turks and the Iranians consider the Kurds terrorists. Let us not forget how we won our independence, and how the British looked on our patriots then as troublemakers. And furthermore, let us recall how in the pre-invasion Iraq of Saddam Hussein, the Kurds were looked upon as no less a bunch of separatist troublemakers.

The Kurds belong to a distinct nationality, and find themselves separated from each other through their dispersal in adjoining areas of Turkey, Iraq, Iran and Syria. At times, they have to cross difficult borders to see their own kinsmen. They desire to be independent in a separate, unified nation which could be created if there is a will on the part of the governments under which they feel separated. They will probably even accept a federated status arrangement with these distinct governments if it was offered to them, and their revolt would subside. But so far there is no will on the part of the Turks or the Iranians to accommodate the Kurds' national aspiration. The new Iraq, on the other hand, has been moving towards a federal arrangement with the Kurds, where they are given enough representation in a new democratic government (which hopefully will last) to satisfy their present aspirations. As a matter of fact, the Kurdish region is the most peaceful area in Iraq at the present time.

The Chechnian and Kurdish problems are a form of nationalism that cannot be labeled as terrorism, even though both groups have performed violent acts of resistance, in accordance with the violent spirit of our time. Similarly, the PLO's actions in the far past, those of Hamas in the immediate past, and Hezbollah's stand against Israel, more recently, have to be considered attempts at resistance against occupation or invasion, a part of national liberation. From time to time violent acts are committed by all these parties, either to bring attention to their plight or as a form of resistance to occupation. The case of Hezbollah, though, is somewhat different from that of Hamas, or the Chechnians or the Kurds. This is because the aspiration of the Shiite community in Southern Lebanon for democratic representation in the Lebanese government has already been met in a peaceful electoral process. The Shiite community is part of Lebanon and the equal representation they desire has to be forged through negotiation alone. Lately, both Hezbollah and the central government have been moving in that direction, and any outside interference in this process by the U.S. and Israel, or by Iran and Syria, would cause an unwanted civil war.

Mention must be made here of the attack on the U.S. barracks in Lebanon in 1982, which resulted in the death of over 200 American Marines. Hezbollah was responsible at the time. That act of violence cannot be excused as anything other than terrorism, because the U.S. Marines were there at Lebanon's invitation for the purpose of helping it achieve peace by ending Sharon's Israeli occupation as well as the intrusion of Arafat's PLO into their daily lives.

So just who is an outright terrorist and who is fighting for liberation from oppression among the Chechnians, Kurds, Palestinians, Israelis, or

Hezbollah Shiites? It would seem that one's view of terrorism depends on which side of the equation one happens to be standing. Both Ben Laden and Saddam Hussein were on our side at one time, and we heard precious little about the terrorist activities they practiced. Such a relativistic view is not airtight, however. It is evident that in certain instances the use of the word *terrorism* is amply justified, such as with Al-Qaida or with what's taking place in the Sudan.

h. Upper Sudan. The civil war in Southern Sudan has been characterized as genocide. The present Sudanese government in Khartoum takes a fundamentalist Islamic position, and has been bent for many years on terrorizing the southern Christian and aboriginal non-Moslem population into either fleeing the area or dying of hunger. In cases of genocide the reasons given for the bigotry and hate invariably consist of rationalizations. It is racial phobia, even though the methods may vary from one place to another, in the use of outright murder, political assassinations, economic strangulation, uprooting olive trees and destroying homes, or to plain daily hard-handed harassment through checkpoints and forbidden movement. It took place in South Africa and in Kosovo, and it is taking place in the Upper Sudan, in Gaza and in the West Bank. The Sudanese government's terrorism borders on a policy of covert racial hate. In all these cases the perpetrators accuse those persecuted of being terrorists when they offer the slightest resistance to their tormentors. That story has been going on in the Sudan for many years now. The plight of the people and the death of children from starvation are appalling—particularly, when the relief food meant to feed the refugees is confiscated and eaten by the soldiers who are persecuting them. The United Nations has estimated that millions have died in the Upper Sudan through war or famine. The terror being spread in this area with the connivance of the central government is state terrorism of the worst kind.

i. The Philippines. Here, an undeclared civil war exists between the central government and segments of the minority Moslem population in the Southern Islands. It has been going on for several decades, but only occasionally does it reach the news. The rebels do commit regular acts of sabotage, just as economically oppressed elements in Mexico, Colombia, Liberia, Nigeria, Uganda, and elsewhere in the Third World have done, more or less sporadically. However, the insurgents in the Philippines advocate a strange form of Moslem fundamentalism mixed with communist ideology, a strange combination indeed which the central government finds hard to accept.

j. Venezuela. The Chavez Rebellion is a most interesting phenomenon which has been long in coming. It needs our attention even though no overt terrorist acts have been involved in its development so far. For the past two hundred years students in Venezuela had been taught that Simon Bolivar's intent in liberating Venezuela, Colombia, Ecuador, Peru and Bolivia (which bears his name) was to unite them together in a United States of South America, in emulation of what George Washington had done in the north. Students are told that through the connivance and machinations of the bigger neighbor to the north, Bolivar's wish never came to fruition. The supposed manipulations of the North are explained vaguely in their texts, but that does not entirely belong to our discussion here. What is important is that they leave their history classes believing that the United States successfully interfered with Venezuela's best interests and killed Bolivar's dream of uniting the five countries he liberated from Spain.

Venezuelan intellectuals—in particular, several political writers and Central University professors in Caracas, known for their leftist leanings—believe that the first arrow shot at Bolivar's vision of a unified South America was the U.S.'s role in sequestering the area of Panama from greater Columbia, of which it was part and parcel. They posit that the Northern big neighbor immediately connived to bring the new Panama (important because of a vision of a canal going through it) under its direct influence, a relationship that has lasted to the present day. It is believed that that very occurrence led directly to El Libertador's untimely death at the age of forty-seven, despairing that his dream of unification would ever be realized. (In all fairness, there are various other reasons for the failure of Bolivar's vision, a main one being the improbability of bringing five hot-blooded Latin countries together in one common enterprise.)

To better understand Chavez, we have to assume that these same beliefs, whether true or not, may have been imbedded in Chavez' inner consciousness since childhood. TIME magazine recently published a revealing interview with him in which he was asked why he believed that his so-called Bolivar Doctrine was replacing the Monroe Doctrine in South America on his watch. Here is his reply:

> For two centuries in this hemisphere we've experienced a confrontation between two theses—America's Monroe Doctrine, which says the U.S. should exercise hegemony over all the other republics in America, and the doctrine of Simon Bolivar, which envisioned a great South American republic as a counterbalance. Bush has spread the Monroe thesis globally in his effort to make the U.S. the police of the world—if you're not with us, he says, you're against us. We're simply doing the same now with

the Bolivar thesis—a doctrine of more equality and autonomy among nations, and more equilibrium of power.—*Time Magazine,* September 24, 2006

And in view of what's happening in Iraq, Afghanistan, Iran, and elsewhere, it is not difficult to see why Chavez thinks that the voracious tiger to the north hasn't lost its stripes over time and would still like to swallow Venezuela and the rest of South America, economically, and, perhaps politically. Right or wrong, what Chavez sees happening with the U.S., from the Middle East to the farthest corners of the world, is its aggressive bent to control all natural resources every where. As he thinks, "What's to stop the American brothers to the North from invading Venezuela and appropriating all the oil and raw iron fields? They went half way around the world to Iraq and Afghanistan to do that!" So Chavez feels that any alliance with North America's enemies may prove to be valuable some day, possibly in the near future, considering the northern neighbor's voracious use of petroleum and all other raw materials.

So, in his interview with TIME, Chavez went on to say that "Bush wanted Iraq's oil, and I believe he wants Venezuela's oil as well. The blame for high oil prices lies in the consumer model of the U.S. Its reckless oil consumption is a form of suicide." Also, to Chavez' mind, a little vexation of the "northern destroyers" of Bolivar's dream is long overdue, and he seems to be enjoying that role immensely. One must understand Chavez's adulation and frequent mention of Simon Bolivar in that light. He aspires to be the new Bolivar. On any visit to Caracas, the sight of the barrios of dire poverty all around the city and the ever present chasm between rich and poor is unavoidable. This has been the case in most Latin American countries for over five centuries. It is their continuing social problem.

Chavez is now giving himself the role of champion of South America's "poor and dispossessed." Dispossessed is actually the wrong term, because for centuries these people never possessed anything. And Chavez sees socialism as the paramount goal:

> After seeing the failure of Washington-backed capitalist reforms in Latin America, I no longer think the same way is possible. Capitalism is the way of the devil and exploitation, of the kind of misery and inequality that destroys social values. If you really look at things in the eyes of Christ—who I think was the first socialist—only socialism can really create a genuine society.

Of course, Chavez ignores the inherent reasons that led to the fall of Communism in Europe, and the debacles that pure socialism has led many nations into, time and again. In 2002, Chavez campaigned vigorously in a referendum that ultimately kept him in power as president. He had thrown in his lot with the poor and dispossessed, and there were more of them than his opponents, the affluent. He doesn't seem to mind that much of Venezuela's capital has already been expatriated to Miami banks and into Florida real estate. The flight of capital from any country should be a cause for alarm, yet in his recurrent speeches he laughs at the fact and proclaims, "Let them take their money out," which makes one wonder about his mental status. He may continue with this attitude as long as the treasury is spilling over from petroleum revenue at this time. Many of his opponents in Venezuela say that the fortunes of Chavez are directly proportional to the price of oil. If that falls dramatically, Chavez will fall from power.

He has imported medical doctors from his friend Castro's Cuba, so that medical care for the poor is available and free. He has since expropriated some oil refineries making oil production a national enterprise. In February, 2007, he did the same with electrical power and energy. To prevent a coup, he has plied the army with wild salary increases to assure himself of their support. Military coups in the tropics are as common as rain. He has aligned himself with Cuba, Peru, Bolivia, Brazil, and distant Iran, Malaysia, Indonesia, and other populous oil-producing Moslem countries. And in 2006, he was returned to power in a national election. That was obviously democracy's gift to President Chavez.

Hugo Chavez mirrors the Sicilian-born Frederick II, emperor of Germany (1218-1250) in his craftiness, flamboyance and rebellious individualism, and in his flirting with certain Moslem countries—that was one side of Frederick's scandalous behavior in all-Catholic Medieval Europe. Chavez understands the plight of the South American poor very well, and sees them living miserably, surrounded as they are by a sea of unbridled capitalism. He is quite aware that the situation serves his own political agenda, and he is playing the role of savior masterfully, worthy of a Machiavellian Cesare Borgia.

Chavez has not resorted to terrorism yet, but he is buying state-of-the-art armaments wherever he can find them. If he keeps up his antagonism to Bush, he may eventually be placed on the U.S. list of terrorists, most of whom are enemies of the status quo. The list is already full of social activists, resistance fighters, and anti-capitalists, all lumped together with a minority of blood-curling and violent bad apples, the few true terrorists. It's a hodge-podge list for which we need a new 18th century Linnaeus, as taxonomist, to compartmentalize it into distinct sub-classes, sub-families and sub-orders, separating legitimate liberation fighters, from confused chronic complainers, and these in turn from the hardened terrorists.

In summary, the problems that have spread like wild fire through the various regions discussed here are only an example of what is proliferating world wide. No list is long enough if we are to mention all the other upheavals in the world, those in Nigeria, Uganda, Liberia, Colombia, Indonesia, Sri Lanka, India, Pakistan, and many other places. The point is that these uprisings and conflicts must be differentiated from one another if we are to deal with them rationally.

Chapter 6

THE IRANIAN PROBLEM: HOW OBDURATE IS IT?

The question is this: Could the American preoccupation with Iran be the result of a state of affairs that has been simmering over decades of suspicion and antagonism between the two countries? Is it a problem that we have created come back to haunt us? In order to answer that question, we must analyze Iran's recent twentieth-century history and study our unwelcome involvement in its internal affairs for the past fifty years.

Iran is an old country that has borne many names and various cultures over its 7,000-year history—Persian, Medean, Parthian and Farsi, to name a few. In comparison we are a young 230-year-old republic. As of 1951 Iran was governed by Shah Reza Pahlavi. Many believe he was a stooge for the British who owned much of the petroleum producing industry in Iran at that time. In April, 1951, the Iranian Parliament named Mohammed Mossadegh as new prime minister by a vote of seventy-nine to twelve. Shortly thereafter, Mossadegh enforced the expropriation of some of the British petroleum assets and introduced other social measures in an attempt to improve Iran's economy and extricate it from British dominance.

Unable to resolve its problem alone, Britain looked towards the U.S. to settle the issue—just as France had done to us a decade later, when we were handed the Vietnam "hot potato." To get the U.S. involved, Churchill's government gave the United States the false information that Mossadegh was increasingly turning towards Communism and was moving Iran towards the Soviet sphere. That was a very damaging spin at a time when the Cold

War was a serious matter to us. Acting on the fears thus created, the U.S. joined Britain and began to publicly denounce Mossadegh's social policies as harmful to his own people. Whenever princes are ready to destroy other rulers, they demonize them first (Machiavelli). And in modern times spin works better for the one who owns the greater propaganda machine and, obviously, we did then, and still do.

In short order, the U.S. administration under President Eisenhower did the British government's bidding and agreed to work toward discrediting Mossadegh by secretly working inside Iran toward his removal. It goes without saying that it was a flagrant interference in Iran's internal affairs by a third party that was not directly involved.

In March, 1953, the CIA, which was headed by Allen Dulles, son of the then secretary of state, was directed to draft plans to overthrow Iran's Mossadegh, for "strategic reasons." Then in April, exactly two years after he came to power, one million dollars were approved for the CIA to use "in any way that would bring about the fall of Mossadegh." Soon, the CIA started to launch a propaganda campaign against him in his own country, through the CIA's agents in Teheran. The Americans and the British were heavily funding the pro-monarchy forces, led by then retired army General Fazlollah Zahedi, a stooge of the Shah (and consequently of the British). Zahedi promptly gained the upper hand on August 19, 1953, and Mossadegh was toppled from power. He was placed under house arrest and later transferred to a military jail. (He died several years later, discredited by the British and Americans, but a hero to his own people.) Following the fall of Mossadegh, and probably as prearranged, Zahedi's new government reached an agreement with the British and other foreign oil companies to "restore the flow of Iranian oil to world markets in substantial quantities."

Two decades later, in the 1970s, the CIA was involved in Congressional hearings about its role in Mossadegh's fall. By that time the Agency's involvement in the affair had become well known. CIA apologists still maintain that the plot against Mossadegh was necessary, and have praised the efficiency of the CIA agents who carried out the plan. In those days one never doubted the "efficiency" of the CIA. It was well run. But many critics since then have maintained that the scheme was immoral and paranoid, and smelled of a nineteenth-century colonial plot. Later, secretary of state Madeleine Albright stated in no uncertain terms her regret that Mossadegh was ousted: "The Eisenhower administration believed its actions were justified for strategic reasons. But the coup was clearly a setback for Iran's political development and it is easy to see now why many Iranians continue to resent this intervention by America." These were courageous words coming from Albright, who, by looking at past history, may have prophetically anticipated what is taking place right now, in 2006, between Iran and the Bush administration.

The interference in Iran's internal affairs did not stop then. In 1979, the U.S., again through the CIA, was involved in propping up its crony, Shah Pahlevi, at the time of the return to Iran of Ayatollah Ruhallah Khumeini. After Khumeini acceded to power, Iranian resentment surged against the United States. At the time, the American Embassy was raided. Many compromising documents of CIA involvement (and of espionage by embassy personnel) were found—just as embassy staff was hurriedly preparing to shred them. American embassy officials were accused immediately of spying on Iran and were taken hostage. That was the beginning of the Iranian Hostage Crisis, which we blamed entirely on Iran. So, for the second time around—the Mossadegh episode in 1953 having been the first—the CIA succeeded in making Iran suspicious more than ever of our motives.

Shortly after, the Iraqi-Iranian Persian Gulf War of 1980-1988 started. The war itself began with Iraq invading Iran, supposedly to recover Khuzestan, an oil-rich province of Iran that Iraq had claimed since the times of Mesopotamia. (Ten years later, Saddam Hussein was to repeat the same claim regarding oil-rich Kuwait, although this time around he had little U.S. backing.) The American involvement in the 1980s' Iraq-Iran war did not start seriously until 1982, under the Reagan administration. At the time, President Reagan announced publicly: "We cannot allow Iran to win the war." So we supported Iraq with arms, finances, and CIA involvement, from 1982 till the end of the war in 1988. As a result, we succeeded once more in antagonizing the new Khomeini Islamic regime, the same ruling party whose accession to power we attempted to derail several years before. And even though we turned against Iraq subsequently—and foolishly removed from the scene Iran's main antagonist—the Khomeini regime has not forgotten or forgiven our animosity during that eight-year war.

The theocratic Iranian leaders have valid reasons to resent our previous manipulative involvement in the Mossadegh affair (1953), the Khomeini episode (1979), and in the 1980-88 Iraqi-Iranian Gulf war. How could they forget all this? Our triple involvement is of recent memory to them. As the adage goes, "Fool me once shame on you; fool me twice shame on me; but fool me a third time and I'll never trust you again!" As things stand now (2006), we say, "We won't talk to *them* because they're sending arms to Hezbollah, a 'terrorist' organization." The more understandable reality is this: "Why should *they* talk to *us*, after we have interfered with their national aspirations three times already, just as Britain and France were doing to them in colonial times?"

The political machinations that went on in 1953 and thereafter should help us understand the present Iranian controversy from a different perspective. Unfortunately, these U.S. machinations continue. Just recently (September, 2006) the UN's nuclear watchdog had to make a stinging attack on the U.S. Congress over an "outrageous and dishonest" report Congress endorsed regarding Iran's nuclear program. The International Atomic Energy Agency (IAEA) complained that a recently published congressional report contained "erroneous, misleading and unsubstantiated information," and that the Agency takes "strong exception" to "incorrect and misleading" claims in the report that said the IAEA was covering up some of the facts about Iran's nuclear intentions. Washington has been trying to ramp up pressure on Iran at a time when Russia, China, the UK, France and Germany—the other main negotiators over Iran's nuclear program—are favoring a more cautious approach. So someone close to the administration fabricates a misleading story.

That congressional report is said to have been written by a Republican staff member of the house intelligence committee who is known for his hard-line views on Iran and who based the report's conclusions on very questionable published material, rather than on real secret intelligence. The dispute is reminiscent of the clashes between the IAEA and Washington (in 2003) over whether or not Saddam Hussein was making weapons of mass destruction, including nuclear arms. The 2003 misleading intelligence report that IAEA complained about then led us into the Iraq war. It was the fabrication of Douglas Feith, a neo-con and pro-Israel supporter, who was embedded in the Bush administration until he resigned in 2005 (see chapter 13).

Iran has no known links with al-Qaida. As a matter of fact, being Shiite, they despise al-Qaida, that Sunni Wahhabite terrorist organization. They will help us uproot al-Qaida if we talk to them—perhaps by apologizing to them first for our constant meddling in their internal affairs! We must talk to them directly, instead of going through the Swiss or other embassies, as we have done in the recent past. In view of the historical facts just described, our hard-nosed arrogance toward Iran is not in our best interest. And our whipping up the American public, using the uranium-enrichment ploy, is unwarranted. Let us stop the Machiavellian way of demonizing our adversary first, before we destroy him. Let us talk to him first, before military action is undertaken which will engulf the whole area in a much wider war.

Talking to the Iranians on an equal footing—whether the Israeli hawks and the neo-cons like it or not—may at the same time solve the Hezbollah dilemma for us and for Israel, and may lead to breakthroughs on many other fronts in our relationship with that large Moslem country. It may even result in a lowering of the price of our petroleum imports. Wouldn't that be a welcome gift for the American driver?

Chapter 7

THE THEORY OF "THE DOUBLE SOLUTION"

As human beings mature, they begin to notice shades of gray—rather than only black and white—in their view of the world and in their dealings with one another. Our predicament of how to define terrorism or patriotism falls in that category. The question then arises as to how do we separate the good guys we want to befriend from the bad guys we wish to avoid? If we use a black and white designation in our relations with all those who disagree with us, like we did when we got into the Iraqi disaster, we (the U.S.) will continue on a road of no-win foreign policy. To the present U.S. administration, the axis of evil consists of Iran, Syria, Hezbollah, Hamas, North Korea, Cuba, perhaps Venezuela, and eventually anyone who does not tow our line. The last point must be emphasized since all of the above countries have declared in plain language and action that they will not allow us to bully them. They disagree with our volatile agenda, and particularly with our bullying role at the United Nations, personified, until recently, by our retiring Ambassador, John Bolton.

So it is important for us not to paint those with whom we disagree in black and those who tow our line in white, or we will continue looking unreasonable and one-sided to the rest of the world. Besides, things in this world are rarely totally black or white. Issues come in all shades of gray. The unexpected discovery in 1924 of a scientific theory, DeBroglie's "Theory of the Double Solution," will help illustrate this point.

For politicians to claim that things come only in black and white—within a field of human activity that is all but exact—is presumptuous and arrogant. Even in the physical sciences, known for their claim to accuracy and exactitude, the explanation for many natural phenomena often turns out to be in shades of gray, and theories held as sacrosanct for centuries are constantly modified by new discoveries. For over two centuries physicists debated whether the nature of light consisted of particles of matter (Newton's view, 17th century), or of waves in motion (Huygens' later view). At scientific meetings they would come close to fist fights, some favoring the first view, others leaning towards the second. And everyone thought the two views were incompatible—until 1924, when a young student at the Faculty of Sciences at the University of Paris, Prince Victor de Broglie, delivered a thesis, *Recherches sur la Théorie des Quanta* (Researches on the Quantum Theory), which gained him his doctoral degree. This thesis contained a series of important findings which first gave rise to astonishment owing to their novelty, but were subsequently fully confirmed by the discovery of electron diffraction by crystals in 1927 by Davisson and Germer. DeBroglie's ideas served to close the divide that had existed in scientific circles for two centuries regarding the nature of light, and turned out to be the basis for developing the general theory of *wave mechanics,* a theory which has transformed our knowledge of physical phenomena on the atomic scale.

DeBroglie had described in that thesis his discovery that light consisted of *particles* behaving (undulating) as *waves.* It turned out that *light* consisted of both! So after years of sticking to a black or white mindset, a novel and enlightened new way of thinking about the nature of light produced a *double solution* which was better able to explain the scientific state of affairs, uniting both sides of a controversy into the single so-called "Theory of the Double Solution." In this manner it came about that both camps—those who held that light consisted of emitted particles and those who were certain that it was a wave phenomenon—were only partially correct. Each of them had half the truth, and when the two halves were combined the whole truth was discovered. All this was thanks to brilliant young DeBroglie's discovery of the "Double Solution."

We should keep this theory in mind when we are involved in internal political debates and, particularly, in our foreign policy disputes. We have less of an excuse to uphold diehard positions in human relations than we do in the more exact field of natural science. Even there, the assured tenets (the certainty) of a nineteenth-century scientific worldview have long ago given way to the indeterminate world of Heisenberg's "Principle of Uncertainty," which postulates that "the simultaneous observation and measurement of two paired quantities invariably leads to unavoidable uncertainty in the results." How elegantly stated is that principle! And how applicable it is to the interaction and differences between two separate individuals (to wit, in marriage), or between groups (political discourse). It is difficult to predict what effect our interaction with sources outside ourselves will have on our perception and attitude towards one another. And that is provided a modicum of reason prevails, which unfortunately, is a rare intellectual commodity in human interaction. (See Chapter 14, Pope Benedict XVI on the use of human reason.)

So why are we mired in negative political attitudes, looking at the world in distinctly separate black and white entities? Must we start new wars of Christians against Moslems, Whites against Blacks, and Jews against Arabs? We will not win a war of the cultures, particularly when we try to paint the whole world in red-white-and-blue American republican democracy. If anything, the other side will win by creating (God forbid) more 9/11 episodes, since they have little to lose and we have ample property and institutions left that they can destroy.

Consider the long waiting lines at airports and the fear of terrorism we are living under. The solution to all this is political dialogue, win or lose; not military exploits to control the mode of life of other people. That must not be confused with pacifism. It is just plain common sense—in contrast to the politics of fear that we are asked to live under. Other nations have a right to self governance and to solving their problems in their own way, free from our interference in their affairs. That desire to control the destiny of others is, I think, the primary cause of terrorism in the world. The use of violence is a counter-reaction to our political and military meddling with, and spying on, everybody and every country. No one, no where in the world, can so much as go outside his home to relieve himself in his outhouse without being detected and photographed by a sky full of our satellites.

We would like to believe that other nations are jealous of us, and thus hate us. No, they are not jealous of us. They despise us for what *they perceive*, unfortunately, as our repeated attempts to force our way of life on them. We cloud their eyes and their minds with those few of our exports which reveal only one side of our life, the worse side: our movies and degenerate music, our moral confusion and subsequent licentiousness, our pornography, and in general our presumptuous immodesty and disrespect for whatever is noble and sacred—the high values which through the ages have been equated with what is decent, holy, and worthy of emulation.

We must not forget that Europe and the rest of the world are even in a worse state of affairs regarding these matters than we are. But the Third world does not consider old Europe or the rest of the world worthy of respect. They have crossed off Britain, France and Europe long ago for having been the purveyors of colonialism and unjust occupation in the past several centuries. They want to look up to us, the United States of America, but are chagrinned by the luxurious waste and the superficial vanity they see in the cultural products we export to them. That is particularly true in the struggling and poverty-stricken Third World.

They know that we were the nation that liberated Europe without occupying it and saved its economic life with the Marshall Plan. They know we are the nation that liberated the Philippines and South East Asia without asking them to sell us their soul in the process. We vanquished Japan, but gave it the power of Western know-how and technology, and even introduced the whole Orient to Western art, music and culture, following their centuries-old isolation and seclusion from Western Civilization. Their appreciation of Western classical music is evident in their high attendance at local performances, in their disciplined musical education, in their astounding production of virtuosi and soloists, and in the sales of classical musical products, which is now greater in the Orient than in the West. All this shows their appreciation of the finer things in Western Civilization and their desire to emulate them and have them—not the fluff we export to them out of Hollywood.

Up to the time of the Vietnam War we were the Third World's idol, the one country worthy of being followed and trusted. They wanted to imitate us, but now they find it difficult to do so. We confuse them by exposing our negative side to them: our militarism, our greed and consumerism, and the bankrupt side of our populist culture.

They no longer notice our historical ability to amalgamate different races and cultures together, Italian and Irish, Black and White, Latino and Yankee, Arab and Jew. Confused by their exposure to our ugly side, they fail to notice how members of our sports teams congratulate, and sometimes hug each other after a game, win or lose. They do not see the good will and honesty of the average American as compared with any other race on earth. No other people have better intentions and a more pleasant way of life, which they have achieved through hard honest work and personal inventiveness. They only see our militarism and our arrogance for being the mightiest power on earth. I wish it were not so. At times, I wish we were a Canada, or a Switzerland, or a Sweden, prosperous, but less inimical to the rest of the world. I wish we would stop looking at other countries only in black and white. I wish we didn't impose on other nations "our way or the highway." I wish we would remember the lessons learned from "The Theory of the Double Solution," and the "Principle of Uncertainty," when we embark on resolving our problems and those of the whole world. I hope we resolve our conflicts with others amicably, being aware that we do not possess the whole truth, but only half of it.

Chapter 8

THE NEED FOR AMERICAN IMPARTIALITY

The world is in need of American impartiality when it comes to resolving geopolitical problems. We must be a nation of resolve, but must avoid throwing our weight in favor of one country against another. Above all, even-handedness must be preached and practiced by both the Administration and Congress—as well as by our news media which has a formidable international reach. The rest of the world is always watching our behavior in foreign policy as it is reported to them daily in publications and on television screens. Everyone knows that Congress predictably and constantly votes or passes inconsequential resolutions in favor of Israel. Congress sullies our image throughout the world when it takes sides and passes resolutions for or against one foreign country over another, especially when it does so to win votes or campaign contributions. If that's the way of politics, it is a shameful and dishonest behavior.

Quite frequently, Congress will vote overwhelmingly in favor of Israel even when that favor goes against acceptable international behavior. By doing so, we exhibit to the world our partiality. Oftentimes, the voting goes against longstanding United States policy—such as Congress' annual vote in favor of moving our Embassy from Tel Aviv to Jerusalem, an act that all our presidents have opposed since 1948. Recently, Congress voted to support Israel unconditionally (July, 2006), while Israel was using its overwhelming air power to obliterate Lebanese civilians and infrastructure. Lebanon was at that time, and still is, our ally. It goes without saying, that all this was readily reported and seen by the entire Arab world on their television screens.

That uncalled-for vote in Congress that went against Lebanon's very survival was unnecessary and politically motivated. It told the rest of the world that our Congress is partial (or bought), and that it will support Israel, no matter what, right or wrong. Why aggravate the whole Arab world for a few local votes or to please the Israel lobby? Under these circumstances, it makes no sense to ask why the Arabs and the entire Moslem world hate us. At the same time, our European allies (and the whole world) were appalled by the pressure we applied to stop an initiative in the Security Council calling for an immediate cease fire in the war between Israel and Hezbollah. That took place even though a literally defenseless member country (Lebanon) was being brutally destroyed by an American-made Israeli war machine, using state-of-the-art American-made weapons of mass destruction (cluster and phosphorus-laced bombs).

The entire South of Lebanon is at present littered with cluster bombs explosive fragments, making huge areas unusable for living creatures or for agriculture. A lesser known fact: Hundreds of kilometers of canals carrying the precious water supply for agriculture in Southern Lebanon were individually and precisely targeted by Israeli bombardment, as if purposefully to ruin the summer crops and any future use of the water canals for years to come. And the beautiful Lebanese coast and its beaches are now polluted with oil spillage from the bombardment of the oil tanks at the Beirut airport. Lebanon is an ecological disaster, and Congress and the President prevented a ceasefire that would have saved the environment from this ecological disaster. Why was this wanton and heartless partiality allowed to take place? To please the Israel lobbies? For the meager campaign contributions they give most senators and congressmen?

This one-sided stance is nowhere clearer than in the use of our veto power in the Security Council to protect Israel from sanctions, whether that country is right or wrong. It is incredible how when a vote comes up in the U.N. to censure Israel for one or another of its frequent *faux pas*, and the rest of the world votes for censure, we invariably invoke our veto power—against the vote and the will of the rest of the world, and always in line with the truant party. It is even more astonishing that the average American is made to believe, through media spin and the administration's apologies that the U.S. and Israel were right and the rest of the world—all 150 nations—were wrong. This ludicrous phenomenon has taken place untold times in the past forty years.

On March 17, 1970, the United States cast its first veto in the United Nations Security Council during the presidency of Richard Nixon, when Henry Kissinger was national security adviser. The subject was the deteriorating situation in Southern Rhodesia (now Zimbabwe). It was a historic moment. Up to that time Washington had been able to score heavy propaganda points because of the Soviet Union's previous abuse of its veto power. Two years later, on Sept. 10, 1972, the United States employed its veto for the second time—to shield Israel. That veto, as it turned out, signaled the start of a U.S. policy to use its veto power repeatedly to shield Israel from international criticism, censure and sanctions.

The initial 1972 veto to protect Israel was cast by George Bush Sr. in his capacity as U.S. ambassador to the world body. Our veto power has protected Israel from censure for violating a broad range of international laws, and has emboldened it to pursue policies that many believe were contrary to its own long term interests. This became clear when a U.S. veto was cast a year later, on July 26, 1973. The draft resolution affirmed the rights of the Palestinians and established provisions for Israeli withdrawal from occupied territories as embodied in previous General Assembly resolutions. That was yet another U.S. veto that killed an international effort to end Israel's occupation of Palestinian lands, thereby prolonging a crisis that has persisted to this day. As mentioned already, the 1970s were the appropriate time to end the Israeli occupation of Palestinian lands, and thus nip world terrorism in the bud. But Kissinger was at the helm vetoing any resolution that called for an end to Israeli occupation—an occupation which has caused us and the rest of the world continual problems ever since.

A later veto struck down a draft resolution that in fact reflected a long held U.S. policy against Israel's alteration of the status of Jerusalem and the establishment of Jewish settlements in occupied territory. Only two days earlier, U.S. Ambassador William W. Scranton had given a speech at the United Nations calling Israeli settlements illegal and rejecting Israel's claim to all of Jerusalem. Yet on March 25, 1976, the U.S. vetoed a resolution embodying the elements of Scranton's speech, thereby, rejecting its own ambassador's proposals, which had been previously passed unanimously by the other 14 members of the council. Of course, Scranton was never heard of again, being dropped from the political scene of his party. He was thus silenced.

Again, under Kissinger's reign, a veto was cast on Jan. 26, 1976, killing a draft resolution calling for recognition of the right of self-determination for Palestinians. Our representative to the U.N. then was Patrick Moynihan. Yet another draft, on June 29, which called for affirmation of the "inalienable rights" of the Palestinians, was vetoed, again under Kissinger's grip on foreign affairs. There have been sixty-eight resolutions passed by the council against Israel since its birth. If the United States had not invoked its veto so often, the record against Israel would total 100 resolutions by now, all condemning or otherwise criticizing that country's behavior in frustrating the rights of Palestinians for self-determination. Could the frequent use of that veto power have been the distant or remote cause of future rebellions, Intifadas, suicide bombing and the other terrorist attacks we have witnessed ever since? As John Paul II said, "Nothing promotes violence more than recurring injustice."

When it comes to the use of spin and misinformation, the power of the controlled U.S. media over the mind of the average citizen is nothing short of dictatorial. Every time the U.N. attempts to censure Israel, our media starts belittling the United Nations, and we use our veto against the will and better judgment of the whole world, when it is attempting to slap Israel on the hand, as should justly be done to a truant child.

Many countries are constantly being censored by the U.N. Security Council, and our representatives give their input one way or another after due analysis. There is nothing new in that. It is part of Security Council business. But the scenario regarding resolutions pertaining to Israel is farcical. It leads to several pertinent observations. First, our unnecessary partiality toward one country over another is observed and analyzed continually overseas. Second, the so-called "free" press participates one-sidedly in this charade, rather than performing its role as a watchdog should, criticizing aberrant behavior by any side in an effort to report the truth. Third, the same media informs us on the spot (to wit, Wolf Blitzer's very "Situation Room") about who's a terrorist and who's a patriot, and often paves the way for governmental thinking regarding these designations. Most reporters overseas do a good job presenting both sides of the Middle East conflict, but the people on the anchor desk (or perhaps higher up) censure what they don't like, thereby making it difficult for the American public to have an impartial view. As of late, the more discriminating individuals routinely avoid television newscasts and get their news from the internet by reading foreign, particularly European, news releases and editorials on the web, and by consulting books written in depth on their subject of interest.

Chapter 9

TERRORISM OR PATRIOTISM: REGIONAL DIFFERENCES

Patriotism has connotations of self-sacrifice, implying that individuals should place the interests of their nation and its common good above their personal and group interests. In wartime, the sacrifice may cost the patriot his life. In this context, patriotism is the reason for the apparent suspension of the instinct for self preservation which we all have—an instinct that suggests that no one would voluntarily serve in a wartime army because he might die doing so. Patriotism obliges one to go against that strong instinct of self-preservation imbedded in all of us.

Patriotism combines two of the four intellectual virtues, justice and fortitude (the other virtues being prudence and temperance). First, justice commands the patriot to do his duty because he owes his allegiance to the group that protects, cares, and defends him when needed. As his country defends him, he is expected to defend his country. That was agreed upon in political writings from the times of Plato, Aristotle, Augustine and Thomas Aquinas up to Hobbes, Hegel and J.S. Mill. Second, a good dose of fortitude is involved, because one has to have the courage to fight for his country even though he is risking his life. On the other hand, prudence, the chief virtue, may dictate the opposite action at times, especially when the citizen sees the conflict as unjust.

Since time immemorial the recruitment of young individuals to man the front lines in battle has proven advantageous, because the young are courageous risk-takers, rash by nature, and short on prudence. They have always made up the frontline of an advancing army. It is also easy to inculcate in them the belief that their group's or their country's policy is the only just one, thus their firm conviction of "my country, right or wrong!"

It so happens that the same characteristics necessary for unquestioning patriotism serve for the recruitment of terrorists. The latter must be young, courageous to the point of rashness, and convinced that their cause is just, all of which causes suspension of their instinct for self-preservation. This becomes more real if there are legitimate complaints against the established order which can be easily inculcated in a young malleable mind. When it comes to terrorism, we are often looking at the other side of the coin we call patriotism. Whatever is the makeup of a devoted patriot is also necessary for the formation of a zealous terrorist. And the "terrorist" may believe in his cause just as strongly as the patriot believes in his, if not more.

The terrorist uses nefarious means to achieve his purpose. He believes that the end justifies any means. The long-held philosophic and religious tenet (diametrically opposed to Machiavelli's utilitarian theories) is that the end does not justify the means. The terrorist may be an individual, a group or a whole nation. There is a similar vein in both an individual group's terrorism and the terrorism practiced at times by an established state (Nazi Germany, Stalinist Russia). We have seen ample examples of both kinds in the twentieth century, particularly when an established state practices mass killings or genocide. Usually, terrorists arise when they believe there is a reason behind their discontent. The reason used may or may not be legitimate; more often than not it does not stand scrutiny and consists of pure rationalizations. But the terrorist is convinced of its validity. That is why it is important to analyze the behavior and listen to the complaints of those we would like to label as "terrorists" to see whether their actions are a reaction to an injustice that can be corrected, or whether their demands are too far out of line and therefore impossible to satisfy.

The Palestinian conflict is a case in point. It is a good example of the kind of analysis that has to be carried out to reach a resolution. There is a definite grievance here: That of an occupation that can be corrected by international pressure on Israel to withdraw to its pre-1967 borders (or adjusted borders) and to give up its quixotic dream of the Greater Israel—a Zionist dream-state stretching east all the way to the Jordan River and perhaps beyond. Behind all the Palestinian uprisings we've seen since 1948, there has been an urgent demand for justice to be carried out in order to rectify their loss of most of their land in 1948. For a long time, that demand has met the silent treatment, if not deliberate obfuscation, on the part of both Israel and the United States.

For 300 million Arabs and more than one billion Muslims the "root cause" of the Middle East conflict is not Hamas or Hezbollah or Iraq. It is rather the festering and ignored injustice of Israeli occupation of the lands that were originally assigned to the Palestinians by the United Nations at the time (1948) of the creation of the state of Israel. As a matter of fact, that was a proviso (a stipulated condition in the contract) in the creation of the state of Israel—in case the world has forgotten. Hezbollah's leader, Sayyed Hassan Nasrallah, recently put it this way, "We arose as a just reaction to chronic injustice."

A further grievance in the eyes of both Arabs and Moslems is the compensation Israel has gotten from Germany for the sins of the Holocaust in contrast to the compensation it has refused to give the Palestinians for their loss of home and land. Until justice to the Palestinians is meted out, the whole world will keep paying the price, as it has been doing over the past sixty years—in high-jacking, abductions, rebellions, and total mayhem in people's lives and property, and to their economy.

We have failed to practice a sense of fairness, as we see editorialized below:

> The rest of the Middle East—and, indeed much of the world, including Europe—regard the root cause of the conflict as Israeli intransigence and arrogance, together with America's blind support for it. In the past few years both the U.S. and Israel have cited foot-dragging in implementing Security Council Resolution 1559, which calls for disarming all non-state militias in Lebanon (Hezbollah in particular), and have called for the deployment of government forces all the way to the southern border. But for years the US and Israel have not uttered a word about the dozens of UN resolutions, going back as far as Resolution 49 on partition in 1947, which called for the establishment of distinct Arab and Jewish states, each on roughly half of the Mandated land in Palestine, between the Mediterranean and the Jordan River.—*The Daily Star*, Beirut, April 22, 2002

The classification of other uprisings around the globe as terrorism, instead of movements of liberation from the yoke of the West, must be meticulously analyzed anew. Even though the globalization of the world complicates the analysis of particular grievances, we must still give attention to the local complaints of injustice, and not confuse them with our global fight with terror (e.g. al-Qaida). Classifying all local movements together with al-Qaida as a form of universal terrorism delays the solution to the localized problems. Both the local conditions and the intent or purpose of these movements must be studied in an effort to reclassify them as separate entities. The majority of troubled areas will be pacified through rapprochement and compromise, even though a few will prove unsolvable—as perhaps al-Qaida may well prove to be. In only a few cases of "terrorism" is military opposition and struggle necessary. And if we are to get anywhere, let's first separate the sheep from the goats and then move on to classify the wolves as a third entity, an altogether different genus. To quote another perceptive *Daily Star* editorial,

> Bush does a disservice to the world and insults his own people's intelligence by mixing together into a single ideological movement and predatory threat what is in reality a range of very different movements, inspired by a wide range of local and global reasons. By linking Iraq, the recent Israel-Hezbollah war, Iran's nuclear ambitions, and Syrian policies as elements in a single threat that must be fought by America's freedom agenda, he highlights a common threat that does not exist in reality as a single, coordinated adversary. This is one reason why he and his administration are having such a hard time achieving their goals in the Middle East, or reducing the threat from terror attacks.— *The Daily Star*, September 1, 2006

The Daily Star editorial goes on to say,

> Bush also perpetuates his misreading of the problem and his ongoing insult to over a billion Muslims around the world by glibly and repeatedly speaking of Islam, fascism and terror in the same breath. This only creates conditions that generate new terrorists among the ranks of wayward and fearful young men living in Arab-Asian societies whose distortions and freak politics in many cases are heavily due to the impact of decades of American [and European] policies.

That is why we must not confuse unrelated issues and must avoid generalizations that lump disparate things together. Many so called "terrorist" groups are fighting to redress local grievances, and do not desire to get involved with our serpentine geopolitical agendas, nor those of al-Qaida. Lebanon is a good case in point. For over thirty years now it has been destroyed, rebuilt, and destroyed again, while being used as a battlefield in a chess game going on between Israel and the Palestinians, on one hand, and the United States and Iran and Syria, on the other. That has been the tragic history of that country ever since Alexander the Great,

2,300 years ago, passed through Phoenicia on his way to India. He laid siege to ancient Tyre, the then Phoenician capital, because it got in the way of his global ambitions. After three months of siege he entered it, massacred all its inhabitants, and burned it to the ground.

Alas, the same destruction fell again on Tyre, in July, 2006, as it was caught between Hezbollah and Israel, on one hand, and the regional ambitions of the United States and Iran, on the other.

Chapter 10

THE PRESENT CONDITION OF THE WEST

The Moslem world often blames Western nations for exporting decadence and immorality across the world. The Moslems point their finger at degenerate movies and publications, immodest dress codes, and the proliferation of pornography. There is some evidence for those allegations. Yet this kind of finger pointing goes both ways. The game of blaming the West for humanity's many ills has been overdone. The West in turn, sees the Moslem world as a breeding ground for idealistic fanaticism, religious intolerance, and widespread practice of polygamy, murder, vengeance and mayhem. Violence is readily used in reaction to the slightest incitement or flimsiest criticism coming from the West. In fact the cult of vengeance, "an eye for an eye and a tooth for a tooth," is preached in both the Hebrew Old Testament and the Koran, the latter having appropriated it from the first. This may perhaps explain the quid pro quo going on constantly between Israel and the Palestinian Arabs. In fact, it has reached the stage of "two eyes for an eye, and the whole body for a tooth."

It was with the coming of Christ that "love your enemies" and "turn the other cheek" was preached as a solution to the tribal antagonism and warfare that had plagued the world for centuries. Prior to Christ, both Buddha and Zoroaster also preached peace and the overcoming of vengeance and greed through detachment and meditation. Christ put it hyperbolically, when asked, "How many times must I forgive my brother, seven times?" The answer he gave was: "Not only seven times, but seventy times seven times." How many Christians, or Moslems, or Jews have practiced that? Only the few canonized saints because they lived up to that Christian injunction. Jesus knew that man is belligerent, unforgiving, and murderous from the beginning. In fact, He was aware of the belief in original sin, which even as a theory has proven to be more accurate in describing human behavior over the centuries than has Jean-Jacques Rousseau's naïve description of the "noble savage" who, supposedly, is born innocent but becomes evil through society's influence. (Incidentally, while preaching the innate goodness of man and laying his corruption at the door of the society he lives in, Rousseau himself sired seven children out of wedlock, and left them one after the other in orphanages across Europe, as he continued traveling far and wide preaching the purity and innocence of the noble savage.)

The present moral condition of the Western countries must be explored because we bear responsibility for the image we project to the Third World. It is indeed an image of sexual laxity and capitalistic greed and their consequences. I say consequences because what we do and what we promote all over the world is based on the capitalistic and Puritan belief that the accumulation of money and possessions is a sign of divine approval. (See Max Weber's *Capitalism and the Protestant Ethic.*) A consequence of this principle is the use of questionable methods to achieve prosperity and success. The way our global corporations operate is based on that tenet. Take the music *industry*, for instance. Music used to be an "art," not an "industry." The proliferation of many forms of hard rock and rap, along with their promotion, and the morally-bankrupt public idols who perform these forms of music, are all part of a major money-making enterprise in Western countries that is being exported all over the world. The same applies to pornography on the internet—the one universal medium of communication available instantly throughout the world for young and adult alike. Is all this being done because of artistic merit and for intellectual improvement, or for monetary profit? How does the Moslem World look at all this, even though in several areas their own practices leave a lot to be desired?

Television, movies and the internet have become the formative media for young people throughout the world, having supplanted the role of religious practice and instruction in our secularized society. How can we preach the Christian, Hindu, Buddhist, or even secularly-derived moral values of gentleness and meekness through hard rock and rap, violent movies, and pornography? If the individual mind is corrupt and decadent, would its representative government lag far behind on that road? Government and corporations only reflect the desires and practices of the individuals they comprise. Suffice it to point a finger at the Halliburton

Company for obtaining multiple contracts during Cheney's Iraq War without the customary bids.

The rest of the world sees all this and points the finger at our casual disregard of common decency—even though they are often guilty of the same behavior themselves. This decadence is not exclusively an American or Western or even a modern problem. It is a worldwide problem affecting even the countries who complain the most about our practices. In fact, even though dishonesty and corruption are found occasionally in our governmental agencies, in many parts of the world the problem is endemic.

Prior to the 1960s, immigrants who came to America wanted in the worst way to become Americans by learning how to speak the new language and assume American dress and behavior. Early immigrants shied away from indoctrinating their children in their own cultural or folkloric past. They would forbid them to speak their native tongue, out of fear of becoming ostracized. They longed to obtain American citizenship and melt into the rest of the population. This was not easy for them, but they worked hard to bring up patriotic American children. But since the change in the immigration laws in the 1960s, the desire to amalgamate has given way to cultural differentiation, to the perceived need to preserve one's ethnic past, and to the cultivation of one's individual cultural identity in speech, dress and looks. Multiculturalism has become the vogue in America and with it, a fracturing of society, a loss of cohesiveness, and a decline in patriotism. Now we have gangs belonging to this or that culture. That has weakened the United States' cohesiveness and its image, both internally and abroad.

Fifty years ago we were envied, both as individuals and as a nation, for our honesty, our fair-mindedness, and our many freedoms. What has happened? Seen throughout our modern world is a decline of respect for the high ideals of virtue and for whatever is noble in life. Part and parcel of the Holy and the Sacred is the life of virtue and the gentility and modesty that go along with it. Such personal qualities that in past eras distinguished the noble from the rabble are disappearing. The distinction between good and evil, between high aspirations and low ones, is all but gone in a pseudo-democratic age, constantly measuring things by ever lower standards—a phenomenon of the advent of the "mass man," as Ortega y Gassett noted in 1932, in his *"Revolt of the Masses."*

For over a century now, we have embarked on a road towards the "standardization by a low standard," a sort of leveling down of the classes and of peoples' intellectual abilities and aspirations towards those of a lower human denominator. There is a silent peoples' "downward cultural revolution," not unlike China's so-called Cultural Revolution of a few decades ago—when the professors, the scientists and the other professional were made to scrub the floor and clean the toilets once a week. Essentially, it is a misinterpretation of the meaning of "equality." Sophocles, the Greek playwright, once said (in a fore-shadow of H.G. Wells), "All the seats in the theatre are equal, but some are better than others."

In a sense, we have lost the higher moral standard in which the world perceived the United States, from the days of its founding until about fifty years ago. We are still more generous, kind, law-abiding and religious than we are perceived to be. Unfortunately, other people are no longer listening to our preaching of equality, democracy, fair-mindedness, and justice as they were apt to do half a century ago. Not that they are any better than we are on the moral scale. It's that they judge us by our partiality and capricious behavior in foreign affairs, coupled with the decadent visual material we export to them. In sum, they no longer see a reason to look up to us. And that attitude is particularly prevalent in the Moslem world. The fact that Japan, and now China, have advanced materially and economically by imitating our methods and our "savoir faire," has little meaning to a devout Moslem. They have their eyes set on Allah's justice and His heavenly rewards. In the long run it may prove to be that their sense of values is more correct than ours.

Chapter 11

TERRORISM AND PATRIOTISM AS RELIGIOUS REACTIONS

Doctrinal religious differences, particularly when dogmatic and uncompromising, will lead to antagonism and intolerance in countries that are unfamiliar with the concept of "freedom of conscience." Saudi Arabia and the Sudan are glaring examples. The reaction of the Moslem (or even the Hindu) fundamentalists to our modern secular view of life is predictable. It is not different from the average believer's view on heretics during the Christian Age of Faith (the Middle Ages). Before the so-called Reformation of the sixteenth century and the so-called "Age of Enlightenment" in the eighteenth, the Catholic faith was strong, allowing little tolerance for deviation from what was considered to be objective truth, as defined philosophically by Aristotle and Thomas Aquinas, and as mandated in Holy Scripture. Perhaps the first principle of logic still is, "a thing cannot, *be and not be*, in the same sense, and at the same time." The Protestant principle of individual interpretation of Holy Writ goes against that principle of logic. It is subjectivism to a high degree, and has in fact led to the division of churches and the collapse of their moral authority, and to the religious wars in the sixteenth and seventeenth centuries in Europe. In those days, the Catholic Church's stance to rebellion in religious interpretation was the same as our present reaction to political revolution. The Church *was* the state. The inquisition tribunals were set up at a time when religious rebellion meant political instability and disorder. There is nothing revolutionary in that method of preserving quiet and order within any state during times of upheaval. In those times, faith meant stability, and heresy represented division and anarchy destabilizing the society.

Where faith is strong disagreement is looked upon with suspicion. In fact, tolerance is a function inversely proportional to the strength of belief. As division and secularism rose in Europe (1789 to the present) religious belief became a subject of greater and greater indifference to a large segment of Europe's population. That is where the West finds itself now. Islam is not there yet. In our day, from a historical point of view, Islam is at exactly the stage of development where the West was in the late Middle Ages (*Quattro-cento*). Christianity then was fourteen centuries old after its founding. Similarly, Islam is now fourteen centuries from its founding by Mohammad. The call to religious jihad is not such an anomaly when religious beliefs are at that stage of development, as evidenced by a study of European history (the Wars of Religion in the sixteenth century, and the Thirty Years War in the seventeenth). What complicates matters even further is that fundamentalist Moslems view the secular state as inimical to religion and faith. They see it as morally confusing liberty with licentiousness and preaching the right of the individual to do anything he likes, flouting all rules and dogma. We increase their suspicion of our "secular democracy" by exporting morally questionable material in movies and on the internet and by promoting feminism and abortion in the Third World. We are blamed for influencing their youth into imitating our Western immodesty in dress, drugs, and general behavior. It is a question of how we are perceived overseas.

It is sad to observe that of the many books written on "the evils of Islamic Terrorism" flooding the market, very few have considered the changes in moral behavior that have taken place in our very midst over the past five decades. We have witnessed a significant revolt against the traditional culture and values of Western society. True, we are in the forefront of industrial progress and we are liable to ask ourselves how could the Moslem world oppose such meaningful progress and not adopt it? But we are also flirting with decadence in the moral realm, and, unfortunately for us, that is what the fundamentalist Moslem sees. We rarely ask ourselves whether we are progressing or retrogressing culturally and spiritually. It is not something that can be measured scientifically. The nineteenth century belief in constant human progress (The Theory of Progress) was celebrated as part of correct thinking for two hundred years before the outbreak of the First World War. After witnessing the cruelty and barbarism resulting from two major world wars we have learned not to equate material progress with overall progress. The fundamentalist Moslem seems to know the difference.

In the meantime, threatening Islam with "crusades," repeatedly speaking of "military options," and discussing our military plans in the open, does not reassure the Islamic world of goodwill on our part. Behavior that appears like twenty-first century colonialism is anathema in every Third World country. Their memory of being under someone else's thumb is all too recent. And frequently, we accuse them of doing to us the things we are trying to do to them, a case of psychological projection. The much ado and hysteria about Iran is perhaps a case in point (see chapter 6).

It is unfortunate that the Moslems in the streets of Karachi or Kabul or Shiraz don't understand what an American really is. They only watch our entertainment exports and judge us by what they see. They shout in the streets, "We want to kill the Americans." Someone in Islamabad publishes in a newspaper the offer of a reward to anyone who kills an American, any American. But what is an American? An American is English or French, Italian or Irish, German or Polish, Russian or Greek. An American may also be a Canadian, a Mexican, an African, or Hindu, Chinese, Japanese, Korean, Australian, Iranian, Asian, Arab, Pakistani, or Afghan. An American may also be a Comanche, Cherokee, Osage, Blackfoot, or a Seminole. Americans are largely Christians, but they could be Jewish, or Buddhist, or Muslim as well. In fact, there are more Muslims in America than in Saudi Arabia. The only difference is that in America they are free to worship as each one of them chooses. An American is also free to believe in no religion if he wishes. For that he will answer only to God, not to a group, or to a government agency claiming to speak for God.

Americans are generous. In the past, Americans have helped out just about every nation in the world in their time of need, never asking a thing in return. They still do. When Afghanistan was run-over by the Soviet army twenty years ago, Americans came with arms and supplies to enable the people to win back their country. Many Americans from various cultures and religions were working in the Twin Towers the morning of September 11, 2001, earning a better life for their families when they were killed by Moslem terrorists. It's been told that the World Trade Center victims were from at least 30 different countries, cultures, and languages. So they can try to kill an American if they must. But in doing so they may be killing someone of their own race or religion, because Americans are not a particular people from a particular place. They are the melting pot of all races.

Yet in spite of this ability for tolerance and assimilation, the United States is targeted by fundamentalists as an object of hate and abuse. There are major doctrinal differences between us and the fundamental side of Islam. We have become liberalized and tolerant in religion; they are still puritanical and judgmental. Their unbending religious beliefs have been a stumbling block for rapprochement between East and West. One of the reasons is that Christianity itself has become more tolerant and accepting in our democratic society. Terrorism of the Al-Qaida type comes about because of the combination of their unbending beliefs aggravated by the partiality and manipulative aspects of our foreign policy. The latter adds oil to the fire of discontent and antagonism.

In some of the Moslem countries, the law or the Shari'a is the last word, a word at times totally devoid of love and compassion, just as it was in the case of the Pharisees and the Scribes at the time of Christ. This is nowhere better illustrated than in the parable of the adulterous women that the Jews were going to stone. They asked Jesus what he would do. He wrote something on the ground, and then said to them, "Let him who is without sin cast the first stone." The stoning (or stabbing to death) of such a woman is still practiced in areas of the Moslem world. By the way, I think what Jesus wrote in the sand was this: "Where is the man who committed the adultery with her?" Wouldn't that be a good question to ask the present day chauvinist enforcers of the Shari'a?

Chapter 12

NEOCONS, CHRISTIAN ZIONISTS, AND BRINKSMANSHIP

Islamic-Western relations, the Israeli-Palestinian problem, and other diverse geopolitical problems are complicated enough without additional intrusion by the agendas of private groups within the United States. Unfortunately, the latter is the case. Peripheral political pressure is brought to bear daily on important state department decisions in order to please one group of lobbyists or another. When the heavy lobbying is concerned with internal affairs, we might say that it is part and parcel of the political process, since in such cases both sides of an issue are usually well-represented by the interested parties. But when the issues belong to foreign affairs, especially those of the Middle East, where one of the parties is never represented to argue its own case, heavy lobbying pressure from one side only raises the question of fairness—and sometimes of the possibility of dual allegiance on the part of the vociferous lobbyists.

These are problems that must be addressed because the stakes are high. The complications that have arisen as a result of these lobbies' direct influence are great and affect the entire nation and the world beyond. According to several reports, the pressure applied by several groups and individuals in high places, especially those closely sympathetic with Israel's agenda in the Middle East, had great influence on the Administration's decision to go to war in Iraq four years ago. Those lobbying elements are still muddying our relationship with countries like Syria and Iran. The influence of the evangelical right on President Bush's decisions and on both aisles of Congress is well known, especially, when it concerns the Israeli-Palestinian question. Equally known is its alliance with AIPAC, the American Israeli Political Action Committee. Their common cause is Israel, but for entirely different reasons.

The role of neo-conservative (neo-con) Paul Wolfowitz—known in some circles as *the architect of the Iraqi War*—was pivotal in our entering that no-win enterprise. Subsequently, Mr. Wolfowitz was made president of the World Bank, away from the political scene in Washington. But pro-Israel groups have covered up his pivotal role in the war. While everyone, from President to Cheney to Rumsfeld have been blamed for the inception and mismanagement of the Iraqi war, Wolfowitz has not, and he was the one who was the most vociferous advocate for that war when he was in office as Undersecretary of Defense.

Elliott Abrams, Richard Perle, and Douglas Feith are three other individuals whose influence on our foreign policy has been detrimental to the U.S.'s best interests. They belong to a select group of so-called "Israel-Firsters," a term referring to those who believe that what is good for Israel is good for the U.S., and when the interests of the two collide, Israel's interest must come first. Feith's connections with hawkish Israeli leaders (advisor to Netanyahu at one time) are well known. Why was he named Under Secretary of Defense for Policy in 2001 by President Bush when he had well-known connections with yet another pro-Israeli hawk, Richard Pipes? For years Pipes had been Feith's teacher and mentor. Both Feith and his father have been honored by the Zionist Organization of America (ZOA), a conservative organization that often makes common cause on foreign policy issues with conservative Christian organizations and hawkish extremists inside Israel.

Feith also co-founded the organization called "One Jerusalem," which opposed the Oslo peace agreement from its inception and has worked hard to undermine all subsequent efforts for peace between Israel and the Palestinians. The original purpose of his organization was to "save a united Jerusalem as the undivided capital of Israel," in direct opposition to the original United Nations partition plan and to many subsequent U.N. resolutions, and in direct conflict with the declared U.S. policy of all previous American presidents. Feith resigned his post on August 8, 2005, when the heat was on him for his part in instigating a war that was in Israel's agenda and in its interest, rather than the U.S.'s. He was found to have deliberately falsified intelligence documents concerning Iraq's supposed connection with Al-Qaida, with the purpose of getting us in a war with that nation, a war that has given us nothing but grief.

News finally broke on Mr. Feith's misdeeds, on February 9, 2007:

Acting Inspector General Thomas F. Gimble told the Senate Armed Services that the office headed by former Pentagon policy chief Douglas J. Feith took "inappropriate" actions in advancing conclusions on al-Qaida connections not backed up by the nation's intelligence agencies. "I can't think of a more devastating commentary," said Armed Services Committee Chairman Sen. Carl Levin. He cited Gimble's findings that Feith's office was, despite doubts expressed by the intelligence community, pushing conclusions that Sept. 11 hijacker Mohammed Atta had met an Iraqi intelligence officer in Prague five months before the attack, and that there were "multiple areas of cooperation" between Iraq and al-Qaida, including shared pursuit of weapons of mass destruction. "That was the argument that was used to make the sale to the American people about the need to go to war," Levin said in an interview Thursday. He said the Pentagon's work, "which was wrong, which was distorted, which was inappropriate . . . is something which is highly disturbing."

Rep. Ike Skelton, D-Mo., chairman of the House Armed Services Committee, said Friday the report "clearly shows that Doug Feith and others in that office exercised extremely poor judgment for which our nation and our service members in particular, are paying a terrible price." Gimble's report said Feith's office had made assertions "that were inconsistent with the consensus of the intelligence community."

White House spokesman, Dana Perino, said that President Bush has revamped the U.S. spy community to try avoiding a repeat of flawed intelligence affecting policy decisions by creating a director of national intelligence and making other changes. "I think what he has said is that he took responsibility, and that the intelligence was wrong and that we had to take measures to revamp the intelligence community to make sure that it never happens again," Perino told reporters.—*A.P. News, Yahoo News*, February 9, 2007

Here is a classic case where a situation, which should have been suspected and prevented in time, came to light too late to avoid a war that should not have been started in the first place. And it is obvious from the report that the Administration still does not understand—or does not wish to reveal—the real culprit or culprits, and refuses to investigate what motives existed for ordering the falsification of the intelligence reports. Now, Wolfowitz, Perle and Feith are no longer in office, but there is still

Elliott Abrams who has Bush's ear. It appears that he's doing everything he can to undermine Condoleezza Rice, now that she is beginning to lean toward a two state solution. Abrams is the most avowed Israel-Firster. It is reported that he gets his instructions from Ehud Olmert and passes them on to Bush as his own. That is not in the U.S.'s best interest.

And what about our erstwhile American Ambassador to Israel, Martin Indyk? He was born in London and grew up in Australia, with a strong Zionist backgroud. He was made American Ambassador to Israel by Clinton, only one day after becoming a naturalized citizen. Who was he recommended by? Feith, Perle, or Wolfowitz? Later he was recalled for giving U.S. policy secrets to Israel. He laid low for a while, then was sent back again as ambassador—a strange situation indeed. Such individuals are a small, but dangerous, minority of the many Jewish people who work faithfully and patriotically for the U.S. government. These "Israel-Firsters" also represent a minority of the Jewish population of the U.S., although they act as if they speak for all of them.

Itzak Rabin, former prime minister of Israel, would often refuse to meet with representatives of AIPAC, because he considered them obtrusive and inimical to Israel's real longterm interests. He was convinced that they represented only the extreme hawkish views of the Zionist segment of American Jewry, thus considering their actions prejudicial to Israel's relations with its neighbors in the Middle East. During his tenure he saw them as interfering with whatever peace process he happened to be working on. Rabin ratified the Oslo agreement with Arafat, and, consequently, was assassinated in Israel by a Jewish extremist, just as was Count Bernadotte forty-five years before him.

Now that we have the Baker-Hamilton Report on our Middle East policy finally out, we might hope that the interference of these groups will not derail that report. It is a well-researched study which advocates, among seventy-nine other suggestions, talks with Iran and Syria, and a speedy resolution of the Israeli-Palestinian conflict. With this report out, many observers feel vindicated for having advocated talks with Iran and Syria long ago, and having insisted on a new American resolve to end the Israeli-Palestinian conflict. One of these is Uri Avnery, a former member of the Israeli Knesset. In 2001, just after the 9/11 tragedy, he felt optimistic that a new awareness of the intensity of the hatred for the U.S. that was spreading throughout the world will finally lead to a change in American foreign policy. His logic was that since the Israeli-Palestinian conflict was one of the breeding grounds of the hatred—if not the main one—the U.S. would make a major effort to achieve peace between the two peoples. He wrote the passage quoted below at that time, hoping for a change in U.S.

foreign policy, a change that never materialized. He thought that logic and prudence would force such a change:

> That was what cold logic indicated. But this is not what happened. What happened was the very opposite. American policy was not led by cold logic. Instead of drying one swamp, it created a second swamp. Instead of pushing the Israelis and Palestinians towards peace, it invaded Iraq. Not only did the hatred against America not die down, it flared up even higher. Instead of drawing the logical conclusion from what happened and acting accordingly, George W. Bush set off in the opposite direction. Since then he has just insisted on 'staying the course.'—Uri Avnery, Gush Shalom, December 11, 2006

George Baker, who wrote the report (along with the involvement of a large bi-partisan group) has been one of the few U.S. leaders in the past forty years who has had the courage to advise action against the Israeli buildup of settlements on Palestinian land. In the 1980s, he threatened to stop American aid to Israel if the latter continued creating settlements. And when they did not stop, he made good on that threat. He stood up to the "pro-Israel" lobby in the U.S., both the Jewish and the Christian right. In his present report he advises the Bush administration (and the public) to extricate the U.S. from Iraq, to concentrate on talking to Iran and Syria, and to urgently start working on solving the Israeli-Palestinian conflict. The report does not say it specifically, but the implication is that peace must be imposed on Israel by forcing them to talk seriously with the Palestinians. The report advises the U.S. government to work urgently on "the final status issues of the borders, the settlements, the right of return [of Palestinian refugees] and the end of conflict." Baker can only offer a recipe; the question is whether the Bush administration will use it. Even if President Bush wanted to follow the suggestions in the report, he will meet strong opposition from vested interests. Here's how one observer sees it:

> It would take extraordinary courage and personal commitment for a U.S. president to halt Israel's creeping annexation of Palestinian land—because of the overwhelming support for Israel in the Congress, in the American media and in Washington's many right wing think tanks; because of major funding by American Jews of both Democratic and Republican election campaigns; and because of the powerful influence of pro-Israel officials embeded inside the U.S. administration.—Patrick Seale, The

Tragedy of Condi Rice, *Washington Report on Middle Eastern Affairs,*
April, 2007

In the meantime our influence and credibility in the Middle East keep sinking to their lowest level in decades. Since 1967, several American secretaries have submitted plans to end this conflict. All of these plans have met the same fate: "they were torn up and thrown in the trash," says Uri Avnery. (Avnery ought to know, he was a member of the Israeli parliament for many years.) Here is what else he has to say:

> The same sequence of events gets repeated time after time. In Jerusalem, hysteria sets in. The Israeli Foreign Office stands up on its hind legs and swears to defeat the evil design. The U.S. media unanimously condemns the wicked plot. The secretary of state of the day [be it Richard Rogers in the 70s, or Colin Powell recently] is painted as an anti-Semite, and the Israeli lobby in Washington mobilizes for total war.—Uri Avnery, December 11, 2006

The fate which sunk the peace plans of these successive secretaries of state confirms the thesis of two professors, John Mearsheimer and Stephen Walt, about the nefarious influence of the Jewish lobby on our interests in the Middle East. These two professors researched and wrote a courageous study that had to be published in England, in the London Review of Books, since no publishing house within the United States dared publish it. It caused such a stir early last year—as if what it reported was something new. According to Mearsheimer and Walt, whenever there is a clash between Israel's interests and the national interest of the U.S., it is the Israeli interests which win. Will this take place again with the Baker Report?

There are ominous signs that it may be torpedoed. The week the Baker-Hamilton report came out, the whole world immediately welcomed the suggestions it contained, except for four predictable objectors who bashed the plan: Ehud Olmert, Israel's prime miniter; Joe Lieberman, senator from Connecticutt; Tom Lantos, a die-hard, Israel-Firster and naturalized Hungarian congressman from San Mateo; and Abraham Foxman, of the pro-Israel Washington lobby. Olmert said, "Nothing has changed. There is no one to talk with, as long as the terrorism goes on, . . ."

The world now views the invasion and occupation of Iraq as a catastrophic failure. Yet one person says it was a success. During a November visit to Washington, Ehud Olmert told Bush, according to a November 14 report in the Israeli paper *Haaretz,* "Mr President, the Iraq war had a dramatic positive effect on security and stability in the Middle East, and was of great strategic importance from Israel's perspective." It comes as no surprise to any observer, that this was a classic example of deliberate obfuscation and the denial of the obvious. A 1996 policy paper by Israel-First neocons who were to be the principal advocates and masterminds of Bush's Iraq war, cited the destruction of Iraq as a major Israeli strategic objective. That wish has been realized: Iraq has been disunited and destroyed beyond recognition for decades to come. Now these same people want us to go to war with Iran. They may succeed in their drive to destroy any country in the region that dares to challege Israel's hegemony. The interests of the U.S. overseas are of secondary importance to them.

It will take another book to treat of the many other examples of this lobby's nepharious interference with our foreign policy. But another danger facing us is the connection between the fundamental evangelicals (now known as the Christian Zionists) and the hawkish Jewish groups in the U.S. The scene of Benjamin Netahyahu, during any of his frequent U.S. visits, giving political sermons at evangelical megachurch halls in the Midwest and the South—all the while discussing apocaliptic Biblical prophesies that he doesn't even believe in—is something very hilarious. As a professed non-believer, he must be laughing beneath his friendly smile when he is allowed to talk about the link between Israel and God's word. To think that he is honestly agreeing with the rapture groups about the eventual conversion to Christianity of all Jews, (and the subsequent disappearance of Israel as a nation of Hebrews,) is the essence of high comedy.

Who are these Christian Evangelical fundamentalists anyway, and when did their movement start? The first American to prophesy the oncoming rapture (a.k.a. Apocalypse, or Armageddon) was William Miller, a born-again Baptist farmer and amateur student of the Bible who lived in upstate New York. In 1830, using the biblical books of Daniel, Ezekiel, and Revelation, he became convinced that the Messiah would return in 1843. He made exacting calculations only to find out later that 1843 came and went and nothing happened. The date was subsequently changed to October 22, 1844, and one hundred thousand Millerites abandoned their farms, sold their homes, left their jobs, and were awaiting the day of hope, the day of the rapture. Again, nothing happened.

Nothwithstanding the "Disappointment of the Messiah not Coming" (the official term they use to describe that episode), a diverse family of denominations and Bible study movements have arisen since the mid-nineteenth century, traceable to the Adventist movement sparked by the teachings of William Miller. These church groups adhere to a strictly literal interpretation of the Bible, with a strong emphasis on the fulfillment of Biblical prophesy in our time. The present day Millerites are the Seventh Day Adventists, the Pentecostals, many Southern Baptists belonging to disparate churches, and several other splinter groups of "born-again" Christians.

Their present importance lies in the fact that they are influential with the present Administration. They believe according to their interpretation of a few biblical segments that the end of time is approaching and, subsequently, that Israel will lead a world-wide war that will end in Armageddon, the final destruction of all nations and the salvation of the few believers left. There exists also, a smattering of right-wing Catholics (William Bennett, for one) who go along with that general picture of support for Israel, and equally base their bias on their interpretation of certain obscure passages in the Bible which supposedly predict the end of times. For Armageddon to occur, they believe, there must be a strong military Israeli machine able to carry on that war. As of late they are tagged as "Christian Zionists." They have been influential in asking for a determined and hawkish attitude on the part of the present U.S. administration, and by doing so have complicated matters considerably through constant interference with U.S. foreign policy in the Middle East.

The neocons, the hawkish pro-Israel lobbyists, and the rapture believers have joined forces for some time now to push for a marked tilt in our foreign policy towards favoring Israel and its political and monetary interests. That has not been in the best interest of the United States. The Christian Zionists tend to be anti-Arab, anti-Moslem, and supporters of Israel, right or wrong. Along with the neocons, they have no qualms about getting us into brinksmanship, as long as they see it benefiting Israel and advancing their skewed understanding of certain passages in the Bible (in *Daniel* and *Revelation*). The leaders in the Arab and Moslem world are aware of the connection between these Christian Zionists and the pro-Isareli neo-cons and, consequently, blame all Americans and all Christians for this obsessive attachment to Israel. Besides, it is not only the blaming game on the part of Moslems that is so worrisome: The greater danger is the advocacy of actual war by these Christian Zionists. Below is part of a long article entitled "Birth Pangs of a Christian Zionism," by reporter Max Blumenthal. The report is quite revealing, yet it is only one example among many others, only the tip of the iceberg of nefarious pressure being applied to skew our already skewed foreign policy. David Brog, interviewed below, wrote the book "Standing with Israel," which included a foreword by his mentor John Hagee, both rabid Christian Zionists. Mr. Blumenthal puts the danger I am referring to in better detail than I am able to present:

> Over the past months, the White House has convened a series of off-the-record meetings about its policies in the Middle East with leaders of Christians United for Israel (CUFI), a newly formed political organization that tells its members that supporting

Israel's expansionist policies is "a biblical imperative." CUFI's Washington lobbyist, David Brog, told me that during the meetings, CUFI representatives pressed White House officials to adopt a more confrontational posture toward Iran, refuse aid to the Palestinians and give Israel a free hand in its conflict with Hezbollah.

CUFI's advice to the Bush Administration reflects the Armageddon-based foreign-policy views of its founder, John Hagee. Hagee is a fire-and-brimstone preacher from San Antonio who commands the nearly 18,000-member Cornerstone Church and hosts a major TV ministry where he explains to millions of viewers how the end times will unfold. He is also the author of numerous best-selling books, like his recent Jerusalem Countdown, in which he cites various unnamed Israeli intelligence sources, claiming that Iran is producing nuclear "suitcase bombs." The only way to defeat the Iranian evildoers, he says, is a full-scale military assault.

"The coming nuclear showdown with Iran is a certainty," Hagee wrote this year in the Pentecostal magazine Charisma. "Israel and America must confront Iran's nuclear ability to destroy Israel with nuclear weapons. For Israel to wait is to risk committing national suicide."

Despite his penchant for extreme rhetoric, or perhaps because of it, Hagee endeared himself to key members of the Israeli right. With the help of former Prime Minister Benjamin Netanyahu, who once spoke at a massive pro-Israel fundraiser at Cornerstone Church, Hagee has raised at least $8.5 million for Israeli work projects. And as a result of Hagee's influence in the Lone Star State, reflected by his enormous wealth—he reportedly rakes in more than $1 million a year from his television ministry—and his close relationship with former House majority leader Tom DeLay, Washington's Republican leadership is just a phone call away.

Hagee recently united America's largest Christian Zionist congregations and some of the movement's most prominent figures—including the Rev. Jerry Falwell, Gary Bauer and Rod Parsley—under the banner of CUFI, creating the first and only nationwide evangelical political organization dedicated to supporting Israel. Hagee says he would like to see CUFI become "the Christian version of AIPAC," referring to the pro-Israel group rated second only to the National Rifle Association as the most effective lobby in Washington.

CUFI's banquet timing could not have been more opportune, staged as Israel and Hezbollah exchanged their first salvos over Lebanon's southern border. While international diplomats were ratcheting up pressure on the United States to administer a cease-fire, Falwell used his speech at the banquet to issue a stern warning to the White House. "I will rebuke the State Department for any and every time it told Israel to stand down and show restraint," he boomed, sending gales of applause rippling through the packed crowd.

The next day, thousands of attendees of CUFI's banquet fanned out to Congressional offices to lobby lawmakers in support of Israel's military campaign in Lebanon. CUFI's lobbying push coincided with the nearly unanimous passage of an AIPAC-authored House resolution declaring support for Israel. Though CUFI's efforts on the Hill certainly did not hinder support for the resolution, CUFI's impact has been felt "on a more subtle level."

Brog explains that CUFI has become a valuable ally of AIPAC, which helps them coordinate lobbying efforts. "They have a great research staff," he said. Brog has also earned the confidence of the Jewish Federation by making sure to elicit the cooperation of its local chapters before initiating a recruitment drive in their areas. "I have absolutely no reservation about working with John Hagee," Houston's Jewish Federation CEO Lee Wunsch told the Jerusalem Post.

More recently, some of Hagee's allies, such as nationally syndicated evangelical radio host Janet Parshall, became ecstatic when Israel and Hezbollah commenced hostilities last month. "These are the times we've been waiting for," Parshall told her listeners in a voice brimming with joy on July 21. "This is straight out of a Sunday school lesson." Not to be outdone, Brog said, "We want to speak to Washington and encourage support for Israel whatever the conflict may be." He paused, adding, "Provided of course that Israel's cause continues to be just." But the renewal of the peace process and rolling back the West Bank settlements would be an unjust cause. For Hagee and for CUFI, all roads lead to a "nuclear showdown" with Iran. Diplomacy would only make God angry. As Hagee warns in Jerusalem Countdown, "Those who follow a policy of opposition to God's purposes will receive the swift and severe judgment of God without limitation."—*The Nation,* August 14, 2006

Such machinations on the part of the few should be cause for concern by the many. The black hole that would result from a war with Iran would be considerably larger and deadlier than is our regrettable mire in Iraq. It would be an Armageddon. Iran is four times larger in area than Iraq, and three times as populous. We cannot allow the religious obsession of a few zealots—a small percentage, outside the mainstream of traditional Christian thinking—to drive the executive and legislative branches of this country on a delusional "prophetic" adventure.

As all this relates to the Palestinian-Israeli question and the resulting inflaming of terrorist elements throughout the Middle East, I quote M.J. Rosenberg of the Israel Policy Forum who explains the problem in his own way (November 10, 2006):

> Forget all the rhetoric about there being no partner. As IPF President Seymour Reich told a press association the other day, "There is always someone to dialogue with. That is if one is seeking dialogue—and we have to be. It's time for some urgency. The situation in Gaza is spiraling out of control. What is the point? Is anyone benefiting from this killing?"
>
> The turnover in Congress could be very significant in this context. The new Congress is far more secular minded than the previous one. So far the Christian Right largely comes to its support for Israel from their religious convictions. They believe that the State of Israel is the fulfillment of God's promises in the Bible . . . . Both Democratic and Republican moderates support the real Israel. As a result, they should be more eager to help Israel achieve a secure peace with the Palestinians. I expect fewer mindless Congressional resolutions which "support" Israel by bashing Arabs. Instead, we may see Democrats and Republicans attempting to work with the President to achieve an Israeli-Palestinian agreement.
>
> It is time for the United States to drop its reticence and to engage in some serious diplomacy . . . . In any case, there is no excuse for the United States to hold back. There is a new Congress. There is a President who says he is ready to work with it to address issues that threaten America's security and the peace of the world. Meanwhile, the Middle East killing goes on, with a new round of suicide bombing in Israel almost inevitable unless America steps in. What, in the name of God, are we waiting for?—M.J. Rosenberg, November 10, 2006, reprinted in *Israeli Insider, Israel's Daily Newsmagazine*, April 1, 2007

It all boils down to the question of whether we have the good will and the willingness to do the job. Is there anyone in this Administration or in Congress listening? Do we still have patriots in government who are really interested in improving our image abroad? Would they have the courage to stand up to the entrenched pro-Israel lobbying groups by embarking on an impartial policy in the pursuit of peace, a policy that is in the best interest *of all of us* in this country, as well as in the long term interest of Israel itself?

Chapter 13

WHERE THERE IS AN HONEST WILL THERE IS A WAY

It is impossible to cure an illness without first making a diagnosis. The illness here is a purposeful form of blindness, called "hysterical" (or functional) blindness. It is a definite medical entity similar to what is known as phantom pregnancy or pseudo-tumor in the brain. Such conditions do occur in people with various forms of neurosis and psychosis; in other words, in those people who have lost touch with the real world. It is to be hoped that the blindness of some groups to the plight of the Palestinians under Israeli occupation is not a deliberate form of functional blindness. I say this because no other foreign subject elicits such immediate hysteria as the criticizing of Israeli mistreatment of the Palestinians, and no matter how disproportionately destructive an action taken by Israel is. Such hysterical reaction to facts may be partially caused by a feeling of guilt on the part of the West towards the Jewish race—the guilt of having been too late to confront Hitler's horrible acts before and after 1939. But Israel is not world Jewry; it is only a Middle Eastern state. Alas, for the Zionists, the two entities are one and the same.

An acknowledged authority on Middle Eastern affairs, the late Columbia, Harvard and Yale Professor Edward Said, once pointed out the following irregularity:

> The only people fighting for liberation from oppression in the past half century that the United States has not cared to help are

the Palestinian people; and that is only so because Israel is their antagonist, and it is cosidered politically incorrect—for both Democrats and Republicans—to critisize Israel, even as it occupies and subjugates another people, weaker than themselves.

The Jewish people are intelligent, hard-working, productive and have in the past been compassionate toward the social problems of others. They are in the forefront of donations to charity and in defending the less fortunate. The majority of American Jews, and about half of the Israeli Jews, do not agree with the hawkish stand taken by the committed Zionists. The ruling parties in Israel and their few supporters in the U.S. seem to be made of a different mettle than the regular peace-loving Jews I have known in my life. They deny having any responsibility in causing the original Palestinians' flight from their homes, and have persisted in their self-serving functional blindness when it comes to the present plight of the Palestinians who are living as locked-up prisoners within their own country. And to add insult to injury, Israel rarely hesitates to attack and kill their women and children inside their aluminum-foil and cardboard-box refugee camps, at the slightest pretext—and pretexts there will always be, as desperately poor people will rebel and riot, as they always have in the past, even under the boot of the most vengeful and tyrannical despots in history.

The partiality of the United States and its people to the formerly persecuted Jewish race is well known. In contrast, there is general public ignorance, and consequent apathy in the U.S., as to the origins and magnitude of the dislocation of the Palestinian people. Suffice it to say that the rest of the world considers our self-imposed ignorance and our one-sidedness in this issue unjust, misguided and dangerous to the well-being of the rest of the world. Even though most Americans are ignorant and confused as to what happened in the Holy Land, the rest of the world knows that starting in 1947, a third party (the Palestinians) who had nothing to do with the Holocaust, had been forced to pay the price for a crime performed by a Western nation (Germany), and have suffered terribly ever since. The origin of the present conflict gets lost among the one-sided verbiage inherent in the reporting of present day events. Precious few in the media mention how it all started, or care to be honest about the past.

In 1952, Arnold Toynbee dedicated a chapter (in the eighth volume of his monumental *Study of History*) to the Palestinian question. The Chinese term for sage (*chihjen*) describes what Professor Toynbee wrote at the time. He was prescient. He entitled his chapter, "The Fate of the European Jews and the Palestinian Arabs." Toynbee wrote this when Israel had been in existence for only four years, and when the plight of the Palestinian refugees was just beginning. I am sure Toynbee never dreamt that another fifty-five years would go by with no improvement—in fact, deterioration—in the plight of the Palestinian people. For the enlightenment of those who are either ignorant, or perhaps care not to know, here is what he had to say:

> The peculiar horror of this confrontation lay in the unprecedented wickedness of the [Aryan] malefactors and the unprecedented sufferings of both innocent Jewish victims and an innocent Arab third party. But the Nazi Gentiles' fall was less tragic than the Zionists Jews'. On the morrow of a persecution in Europe in which they had been the victims of the worst atrocities ever known to have been suffered by Jews or indeed by any other human beings, the Zionists' immediate rection to their own experience was to become persecutors in their turn, at the first opportunity that had since arisen for them to inflict on other human beings who had done them no injury, but who happened to be weaker than they were, some of the wrongs and sufferings that had been inflicted on the Jews by their many successive Western Gentile persecutors during the intervening seventeen centuries. In A.D. 1948 some 684,000 out of some 859,000 Arab inhabitants of the territory in Palestine which the Zionist Jews conquered by force of arms in that year, lost their homes and property and became "displaced persons." This impulse to become a party to the guilt of a stronger neighbor by inflicting on an innocent weaker neighbor the very suffering that the original victim had experienced at his stronger neighbor's hands was perhaps the most perverse of all the base propensities of Human Nature. The tidal wave that overwhelmed the Palestinian Arabs in 1948 was a backwash from an upheaval in the relations between Gentiles and Jews in Western longitudes beyond the Palestinian Arabs' horizon.—Arnold Toynbee, *A Study of History*, vol. VIII, pp. 288-312

The magnitude of the dislocation which occurred then, is barely glossed over now, sixty years later. Time sooths bad memories. But Toynbee was writing a mere four years after all this occurred and the memory of the horrendous injustice that took place then was still fresh in everyone's mind. Professor Toynbee goes on to indict Great Britain and the United States for their responsibility in the catatrophe that overtook the Palestinians (the Palestinians call it the *nakbeh*, in Arabic, meaning the *disaster*):

> In 1948 there was no power on earth strong enough to say nay to Western Society when the western victors in the War of 1939-45 chose to compensate the Western Jews for the crimes committed

against them by a defeated Western belligerent [Germany] at the expense, not of the guilty West, but of an innocent non-Western people. In its impotence to resist this injustice the rest of Mankind could only marvel at Western Man's attempt to obtain absolution for a Western sin by imposing a proportionate penance on strangers who were not implicated in the guilt . . . While the direct responsibility for this calamity that overtook the Palestinian Arabs was on the heads of the Zionist Jews who seized a Lebenstraum for themselves in Palestine by force of arms, a heavy load of indirect, yet irrepudiable, responsibility was on the heads of the people in the United Kingdom; for the Jews would not have had in A.D. 1948 the opportunity to conquer an Arab country in which they had amounted to no more than an inconsiderable minority in 1918 if, during the intervening thirty years, the power of the United Kingdom had not been exerted continuously to make possible the entry of Jewish immigrants into Palestine contrary to the will, in spite of the protests, and without regard to the forebodings of Arab inhabitants of the country who in 1948 were duly to become the victims of this long pursued British policy . . . Another factor was the rise of the Jewish community in the United States to a great degree of economic and political power in American life . . . so that the Democratic and Republican parties vied with one another in contending for Jewish support by displaying a competitive zeal for furthering the fulfilment of Zionist aspirations. (*A Study of History*, vol. VIII, pp. 288-312)

This was the insight of the twentieth century's greatest historian in 1952, when Israel's continued existence was not so certain as it is now, and when the memory of the land expropriation from the Palestinians was still too fresh in everyone's mind to be forgotten. As a philosopher of world history, and with great psychological insight, he knew that what was happening then would cause chaos in the Middle East's balance of power for decades to come. Of course, now we would not even think of questioning Israel's existence; indeed its nationhood is a fact of life, because our minds are numb to what took place so long ago (between 1918 and 1948). And granted that Toynbee's analysis is harsh, and his equating of the millions of Jews killed under Hitler with the fate of 600,000 or more Palestinian refugees is disproportionate; yet he shows how people felt when the memory of the unexpected event was fresh in their mind, compared to our present-day repeated attempts to ignore or cover up what happened then. And he wrote this before the expropriation and expatriation of an additional million

Palestinian refugees during the future wars of 1967, 1973, and the various intifadas, up to the present.

That segment of the American public who keeps repeating, "Oh! They've been fighting forever," are utterly unaware of the United States' and Britain's responsibility in creating the present seemingly unsolvable carnage. If there is any shred of honor or good will on the part of Israel, an official apology to the Palestinians should be made, just as past Popes have apologized for the Crusades, for the Inquisition, and for the Galileo case. A mere apology would make it easier for the Palestinians to accept their suffering and Israel's de facto existence, not only verbally but emotionally as well. And hopefully, Israel or the Western powers would then make reparations similar to the way Germany has performed toward Israel since 1945. But there is little good will towards the Palestinians to be found in Western consciences, and Israel's disproportionately harsh treatment of the Palestinians (and of their leaders) shows no compassion whatsoever towards the people whose land they have taken and occupied. At present, the Palestinians are, economically and politically, destitute prisoners within a land that was theirs for millenia.

There is one superpower that can lead both sides to a permanent peace, and that is the United States. There appears to be now a rising willingness on our part to do that. I hope it will not be derailed. But any amount of good will engendered must come at this juncture from the Israeli people themselves. In this regard, they must not expect any encouragement from their Jewish American cheerleaders. The large number of Brooklyn orthodox Jews that leave their American homes and their prosperous way of life to immigrate to Israel and set up settlements in an arid area of the West Bank definitely complicate the quest for a solution and increase the dispossession of the Palestinians. If anything, they inflame both sides who are trying to achieve peace. The same can be said about the Palestinian suicide bombers of the past, and the ineffectual rocket attacks the Gazans carry on across the demarcation line. The other Arabs (Egypt and Jordan) have been offering their help toward reconciliation for years. Suicide bombers and Intifadas have not promoted good will, but neither has Israel's disproportionate military response over the years, nor its building of an internationally-unsanctioned wall on Palestinian land, thus shutting itself from contact with the Oriental World.

We will not achieve peace without a good will that leads to justice. We in the U.S. must also learn to quiet down our statements of invective against Arabs and Moslems, and must take care not to dumb down Moslems and Arabs in general, or the Palestinians, in particular. It is interesting that as of late we have been calling the so-called terrorists in Iraq "insurgents." At the very least, let us also start to refer to the Palestinian resistance fighters as "insurgents" (and not as "terrorists"), as they are fighting to free their country from a cruel occupation.

The same priciples against name-calling should be applied to the many regional conflicts around the globe, such as Chechnia, Kurdistan, the Philippines, and the problematic presidency of Chavez. Contacts and dialogue are possible and mandatory. For Chechnia and the Kurdish problem, federation or independence are not impossibilities, provided there is good will on the part of the larger entities involved. However, we must also understand that within any sovereign country a stage is reached when a nation cannot accommodate every request of every minority. The United States can lead the way in that regard because of our national experience. As a union of states we are natural experts on that subject. And when it comes to racial minorities, we have come a long way in dealing with our racial problems. We have demonstrated at least that dissimilar races and nationalities can live together and thrive in a modicum of peace and harmony.

The opposite example is Sudan. There, an ill-willed fundamentalist Moslem government is bent on social cleansing. Nothing short of United Nations peacekeepers will solve that problem. Venezuela's Chavez may be ready to subsidize many rebellions in the South American and Carribean countries if we don't begin a serious dialogue with him. His invective, justified or not, must be a matter for the U.S. State Department, not the CIA. Humility and an appeal to friendship are necessary on our part or a second problematic Middle East may come about in our hemisphere.

There is too much poverty in Latin America because of unbridled capitalism and government corruption. This may very well be a problem for the individual countries to solve, but with Chavez around, it will soon turn out to be a hemispheric problem. Early realization and resolution are of the utmost importance here. We must not allow our obsession with Iraq and Iran to take over our concerns toward South America, an area much closer to us. Again, direct contact with rebellious Chavez on the part of the United States will save the day. Members of the opposition parties in Venezuela believe that Chavez, with his penchant for celebrity attention, would welcome a request for dialogue from President Bush.

Chapter 14

POPE BENEDICT XVI ON THE USE OF REASON

In the fall of 2006, the world was perplexed and shaken by a lecture given by Pope Benedict XVI to professors and students at the University of Regensberg in Germany. The Pope was addressing a philosophical question concerning the relationship between faith and reason. This is a fundamental inquiry that arose with the founding of Western European universities in the twelfth and thirteenth centuries. The question then was the compatibility of truths derived by human reason (the philosophy of Plato and Aristotle) with the truths taught by religion through faith (Holy Scripture). In essence it had to do with the relationship between philosophy and theology since these were the two main subjects taught in universities at that time. These were also the centuries when Islamic learning in philosophy, theology and science was at its apogée.

The Pope was quite aware of Al-Qaida's link to Moslem fundamentalism, and equally cognisant of the problematic fanaticism which that linkage has presented to the modern world. The Moslem fundamentalist's intolerance of other religions and innate opposition to freedom of conscience has created a world-wide problem. The question is whether intolerance and forceful conversion are proscribed in the Koran (Qur'an). The Holy Book is indecisive about the subject. Under some readings, it would put pagans to the sword for not converting to Islam. Some linguistic experts believe it is more forgiving towards the "people of the book" (Jews and Christians). Other experts, however, disagree: Coversion may come at the point of a sword. For this reason, freedom of conscience as we know it in the West, is nebulous, if not outright rejected in many areas of Islam. That is most obvious in the religious policies within Saudi Arabia and the Sudan, but less so in several other Moslem countries. For example, in Syria, a predominantly Moslem nation, freedom of religion between Moslems and Christians is accepted. That was also the case in Iraq under the secular governance of Saddam Hussein.

In his address at Regensburg, Pope Benedict XVI questioned any religion's use of violence as a conversion tool. He suggested that the use of human reason and dialogue could form a bridge of understanding between the various religions. The Pope showed great courage and foresight in trying to start a dialogue with Islam on the subject of religion and violence by opening up the questions of religious tolerance and free conscience. To achieve that, he purposely raised the question of the dual importance of both faith and reason in theology. The Pope was familiar with this philosophical question and knew full well that it had been raised and solved long ago in the Christian West. During the thirteenth century, St. Thomas Aquinas wrote extensively about the subject, interestingly enough, in answer to the teachings of the Moslem philosopher Averroes who claimed that faith and reason may hold irreconcilable opposing truths.

Aquinas' entire *Summa Contra Gentiles,* and later his several volumes of the *Summa Theologiae,* were written to show that a thorough analysis of what faith teaches is not incompatible with reason. His conclusion was that the tenets of faith are just another form of information, a revealed and refined spiritual information, not incompatible with, but complementary to, the truths found by the use of human reason. In fact, Aquinas (1225-74) and his Dominican Order championed the use of reason during the height of the Age of Faith. In 2006, the Pope reintroduced that concept with a twist: A religion based only on its own Holy Scripture also must use reason if it is to dialogue with other religions. Otherwise, no communication is possible. He was goading not only Islam on that point, but also Christian fundamentalists and the secular world's relative humanism, both of which, in their own way, deny the power of human reason.

In challenging Fundamental Protestantism, Pope Benedict was buttressing two of the three pillars that Protestantism had rejected and which had sustained Christianity for fifteen centuries before it, and five centuries since. He was referring to Christianity's debt to Greek reason and philosophy, as well as to the order and organization which the Church derived from Roman Law. He pointed out that both of these influences were ancillary additions to the Hebrew biblical tradition that is at the heart of Christianity. He was thus indirectly proposing to the fundamentalists that the third pillar, the Bible (even as God's word), cannot stand alone in the dialogue with other religions. Different religions claim different Holy Books (and therefore different "words" of God). But the human faculty of reason is common to all. For this reason, the Catholic Church has always stressed that a strictly literal interpretation of any holy scripture frustrates rapprochement between different religious traditions and cuts off valuable communication because it eliminates the use of universal truths—that is, principles common to both faith and reason.

In essence, the Pope was extolling the use of reason as a bridge of communication between different faiths. Of course, the news media missed that point. Instead, the media fixated on his quotation of a fifteenth century Pope who called the Islamic faith "evil and inhuman"—and the susequent reaction of many Muslims to his quotation. But in doing so, the media still missed the Pope's main message to Islam: that to dialogue with the West Islam must use reason and logic, as well as common beliefs, and it must renounce the violence emanating from strict fundamentalism. He was implying that until that occurs, "East will remain East and West will stay West, and the twain will never meet." Alas, in our age of globalization and instant information, isolation is not possible and we must necessarily encounter each other without violent confrontation. Scientific, commercial and cultural meetings of the mind have become daily occurrances between East and West. The Pope wanted to likewise encourage religious meetings of the mind. As a trained professor of both philosophy and theology, he was speaking as an expert on the old subject of faith and reason. It is unfortunate that most of the world media, along with Islam and the Christian fundamentalists, failed to understand his intellectual depth and the subtlety of his philosophical discourse.

The questions raised and the solutions offered by the Pope concerning the use of dialogue based on human reason, pertain just as much to the Israeli-Palestinian impasse as to the the Christian-Moslem dialogue. Dialogue occurs only when communication is constant and when good will and impassionate reason are prevalent in place of emotional reaction and recrimination. Problems can be solved using dialogue and reason, with good will on both sides, rather than through military confrontation.

Chapter 15

WORKING TOWARDS A PEACEFUL WORLD

Living on earth in uninterrupted peace and tranquility is hardly possible for individuals, let alone for nations. Any expectation of Nirvana on this planet is apt to disappoint the wishful planner. That is why Utopias written over the centuries by well-meaning authors gather dust on bookshelves. This earth is not heaven, nor will it ever be. Human beings are psychological and emotional creatures whose actions are difficult to predict and control. Notwitstanding, intervals of peace have occured in human history, and a few have lasted a hundred years or more (e.g. the *Pax Romana,* 98-180 A.D.). So we must not despair of working for peace in our time.

    Thomas Aquinas, the medieval scholar and saint, gave the same definition to the concept of peace that he did to philosophical (and scientific) inquiry. He defined both as the "tranquility of order." He was referring to the fact that for peace and sanity to exist there must be tranquility of mind through knowledge of the natural order of things, so that we humans do not misuse them. This means an acceptance of the difference present in living creatures and in created things, each one organized in its order of place and category. In other words, each individual thing has a function derived from and natural to the way it was constructed, and in turn belongs to a certain class of objects of similar function and construction. The structure and function of an object or creature must not be taken out of their natural order of being (that is, they must not be perverted, or put to the wrong use).

It is not natural to open a door with a sewing needle, although one may try; nor is it practical to use a house key to sew a garment. Each implement has its individual structure, designed to perform a specific function. Problems arise when free humans and free nations confuse or reverse the order of things, in their mind and in public discourse. Wars occur when nations covet each other's land or prerogatives and break their promises and contracts, essentially, when they abuse and pervert the order of things.

The same idea of order applies to knowledge, to the disciplines of philosophy, theology and the natural sciences. *Philosophia,* the love of wisdom, is perfected by the knowledge of the order of things and the ability to keep them within the categories to which they belong. Prudence in daily living, as in politics, would be absent if things were disorganized, not kept in order. The tranquility of society would be disturbed if things were in disarray. It all comes down to the ability or willingness to know how to keep things, or thoughts, or ideas, in their order of place and time. For Aquinas, as for Pope Benedict, to create order is divine work (like the universe); confusion is the work of Satan.

In the same vein, and keeping in mind the concepts of *ordering* and *categorizing* when it comes to the subject of "terrorism or patriotism," we must realize the similar bent for destructiveness inherent in both: the "terrorist acts" carried on by individuals or groups, and the "hyper-patriotic or chauvinistic" agression and persecution undertaken by sovereign states. But, no less important is our acknowledgement of a decided difference existing between: (1) "Liberation movements," or armed attempts at liberation in occupied lands, from (2) "Pure terrorism" motivated by anger and hate, or cultural and religious intolerance, such as with Al-Qaida and similar movements. Besides, some movements are localized, specific, and easier to deal with. Others are amorphous, nebulous and generalized, quite difficult to solve. Thus, there exists a whole spectrum of reactionary violence that we must place in distinct groups, if we are to deal with them successfully.

Let us not forget that the British looked on the early American patriots as terrorists, or at the least, as insurgents and listed them as unfaithful traitors to the crown. We must abandon the temptation to lump all rebellions and uprisings together under the catch-all, heavy-laden term of "terrorism." When we do so, we sin against "the tranquility of order." Likewise, we will never have peace in our time, if we condone or tolerate the forced acquisition of other people's lands, whether done by a sovereign state or by individuals. There is a limit to both, the violent acts of freedom fighters and the greed for conquest (and the desire for control) we witness in the actions of sovereign states.

An attempt at categorizing the various terrorist and resistance movements was made in the previous chapters. The causes or reasons behind some of them were explored. The concepts of terrorism and patriotism were dicussed. Suggestions for a solution to each have been presented in general, but less so in specifics, as that would belong to diplomatic dialogue and negotiations. Suffice it to say that experts may disagree on the proper order of procedures and on the order of their undertaking, but it is imperative that we begin the task of dealing first (and one by one) with the solvable problems of liberation movements. Then, the more generalized and, perhaps, mindless forms of terrorism can be sequestrated from the rest and dealt with firmly and agressively. Above all, we must remain humble and patient, knowing that we cannot solve all the problems of the world, at least not all at once. A good dose of good will and openness in dialogue, and a reduction in the use of Machiavellian tactics by both individual groups and sovereign states, will take us a long way towards the goal of peace in this world during the rest of this century.

* * *

Bibliography

Alan, Curtis, *Patriotism, Democracy, and Common Sense*; Rowman & Littlefield Publishers, 2005

Altheide, David L., *Terrorism and the Politics of Fear;* Alta Mira Press, 2006

Baer, Robert, *See No Evil: The True Story of a Ground Soldier in the CIA's War on Terrorism*; Three Rivers Press, 2003

Bjorgo, Tore, *Root Causes of Terrorism: Myths, Reality, and Ways Forward;* Routledge, 2005

Bovard, James, *Terrorism and Tyranny, Trampling Freedom, Justice and Peace to Rid the World of Evil*; Palgrave McMillan, 2004

Brzezinski, Zbigniew, *Second Chance, Three Presidents and the Crisis of American Superpower*; Basic Books, March 5, 2007

Buckley, M. and Singh R., *the Bush Doctrine and the War on Terrorism: Global reactions*; Routledge, 2006

Carter, Jimmy, *Palestine, Peace or Apartheid*; Simon and Schuster, 2006

Chomsky, Noam, *Failed States*; Henry Holt & Company, 2006

Crenshaw, Martha, ed., *Terrorism in Context;* Pennsylvania State University Press, 1994

Dreyfuss, Richard, *Devil's Game, How the United States Helped Unleash Fundamentalist Islam*; Metropolitan Books, 2004

George, Alexander, ed., *Western State Terrorism*; Polity Press, 1991

Hastings, Tom H., *Nonviolent response to Terrorism;* McFarland & Company, 2004

Levi, Margaret, *Consent, Dissent, and Patriotism*; Cambridge University Press, 1997

Martin, C. Gus, *Understanding Terrorism: Challenges, Perspectives and Issues*; Sage Publications, Inc, 2006

Mearsheimer, John J. and Walt, Stephen M., *The Israel Lobby and U.S. Foreign Policy*; London Review of Books Vol. 28, No. 6 (March 23, 2006), available online at www.lrb.co.uk

Mickolus, Edward, ed., *the Literature of Terrorism, a Selectively Annotated Bibliography*; Greenwood Press, 1980

Moghaddam and Marsella, editors, *Understanding Terrorism: Psychological Roots, Consequences, and Intervention*; American Psychological association, 2003

Nassar, Jamal R., *Globalization and Terrorism, the Migration of Dreams and Nightmares*; Rowman and Littlefield, Publishers, 2004

Neff, Donald, *Fallen Pillars, U.S. Policy towards Palestine and Israel since 1945*; Institute of Palestine Studies, Washington, D.C., 1995

Norris, Kern, and Just, editors, *Framing Terrorism: The News Media, the Government, and the Public*; Routledge, 2003

Parenti, Michael, *The Terrorism Trap, September 11 and Beyond*; City Lights Publishers, 2002

Perdue, William D., *Terrorism and the State, a Critique of Domination by Fear;* Praeger Publishers, 1989

Pillar, Paul R., *Terrorism and U.S. Foreign Policy*; Brookings Institution Press, 2003

Reich, Walter, ed., *Origins of Terrorism, Psychologies, Ideologies, Theologies, States of Mind*; Woodrow Wilson Center Press, 1998

Rokash, Livia, *Israel's Sacred Terrorism: A Study Based on Moshe Sharett's Personal diary and Other Documents*; A-A Univ. Grad., 1985

Said, Edward, *The Politics of Dispossession*; Vintage, May 30, 1995

Shlaim, Avi, *The Iron Wall*; Norton and Company, 2000

Sizer, Stephen, *Christian Zionism, Road Map to Armageddon?*; IVP Academic, 2004

Sterba, James P., ed., *Terrorism and International Justice*; Oxford University Press, USA, 2003

Tolstoy, Leo, *War, Patriotism, Peace*; University Press of the Pacific, 2002

Toynbee, Arnold J., *A Study of History*, Vol. VIII; Oxford University Press, 1952

Wagner, Donald E., *Dying in the Land of Promise, Palestine and Palestinian Christianity from Pentecost to 2000*; Association of Arab-American University Graduates, 2005

Wagner, Donald E., *Anxious for Armageddon*; Herald Press, 1995

Biography Of The Author

Dr. Hensley J. Hunter was born to American parents working in the Middle East following the end of World War I. He attended schools in Beirut and Damascus, learned French and Arabic, and later went overseas for graduate studies. He completed his postgraduate work in London where he obtained his doctoral degree. His life defies typecasting—he is a devout Christian who loves his Jewish and Islamic brothers and ardently desires to see peace come between them during his lifetime; he is a conservative Republican who passionately opposes current Republican foreign policy on all counts. His expertise lies in the history of the Israeli-Palestinian conflict during the past century. For fifty years, he has traveled extensively to the Middle East and Africa to familiarize himself with problems of the Third World. Dr. Hunter's main interest, however, remains the Middle East. His wide experience and knowledge of that region is manifest in *Terrorism or Patriotism*, a welcome primer on understanding the Middle East conflict.

Printed in the United States
132439LV00014B/184/A